Dating Tl

Building a Winning Relationship
With Your Desires

◆

Wes Beavis

POWERBORN
Los Angeles ◆ Sydney

<u>DATING THE DREAM</u>
Building A Winning Relationship With Your Desires
by Wes Beavis

1st Printing 1996

ILLUSTRATIONS BY
Keith Poletiek

COVER ILLUSTRATION BY
Keith Poletiek
Drew & Nancy Ward

PUBLISHED BY
The Catalyst Group
1 Berghem Mews
Blythe Road
London W14 0HN
Tel: 0171 603 7779 Fax: 0171 603 2220

Beavis, Wesley James, 1962—
    Dating The Dream—Building a Winning Relationship With
Your Desires/ Wes Beavis
        p.   cm.
    ISBN 0-952 7437-2-8
    1. Success in business—United States.   2. Quality of life—
United States.   3. Work & Family—United States.
    4.   Self-actualization / maturation (Psychology) I. Title
        158.1 BEA —dc20   1996
    Library of Congress Catalog Card Number 96-67239

Printed and bound in Great Britain by
Redwood Books, Trowbridge, Wiltshire

Dedicated to
David Lincoln & Zachary James

— Special Thanks To —

Eleanor
Rebecca Avery
Scott Alexander
Ed Masters

CONTENTS

INTRODUCTION

◆

> People who build a good relationship
> with their desires are more likely to
> achieve them.

THE OCCASION WHEN I first saw her was quite dramatic. I had been outside taking a leisurely walk when the serenity was interrupted by the stomach wrenching sound of crumpling metal and falling glass. Two cars had fought over the same piece of road. Neither had won. My arrival on the scene was just moments after the impact. Thankfully, no one was seriously hurt but there was still enough reason to have a fleet of ambulances tending to the injured.

Then I saw her. Assisted by paramedics, she emerged from a mangled car and laid down on a stretcher. The gash on her forehead and the anguished look on her face was not enough to conceal her profound beauty. She was the most attractive woman I had ever seen. In that moment, she looked so vulnerable and my heart went out to her. It is hard to explain, but feelings of love came out of nowhere. I had found the one I wanted to marry. It was easy to imagine, from that moment onward, this girl and myself being together always.

Yet, though I desired it, the marriage never took place. Two things stopped it. I never did actually meet her. And being ten years old at the time, my age hampered the possibility.

Putting aside the aspect of my youth, it was inevitable that I did not get what I desired. There was no relationship with *whom* I desired.

Getting what you desire demands building a positive relationship with what you desire in the first place. This is something many people fail to do and thus their desire is really just as wishful as the matrimonial desires of an infatuated ten-year old.

I was told recently that a survey taken in the United States brought to light the statistic that 76% of all working people disliked their jobs. Can you fathom that? Seventy-six people out of every hundred are wasting their one chance at life by doing something other than what they would prefer to be doing. What a tragedy, especially since most of these people would admit to having a desire for a more satisfying working life.

Why doesn't desire alone propel people out of a dissatisfying existence? The answer is because their desire is no more than wishful thinking and wishful thinking has very little motivating power within itself.

Really there is no difference between wishful thinking and desire if a person does not establish a relationship with their desire. It is the quality of how we relate to what we desire which lifts our desire out of the 'wishful thinking' status.

The power that a desire has to motivate us grows in strength the more we build the relationship with what we desire.

Building a relationship with a special desire is very much like building a relationship with a special person. There are specific stages that you go through as the relationship matures. In relating to another person, you find the strength of the relationship intensifies as you go from one stage to the next. Successful transition through the stages can turn a person in your life to a partner for life.

It is the same when considering how you relate to a desire. Moving through the stages turns a desire in your life to a destiny for your life.

This is what this book is all about. Helping you to build a *winning* relationship with your desires.

So, here's to dating *your* dream, a great relationship in the making.

Let's commence with Stage One . . .

◆

Stage 1

Sorting Through the Attractions

(What Love is This?)

◆

> *Building a winning relationship with your desires starts by wanting success in every field of your life, not just one field.*

"I'M SORRY, he's not available to speak to you. He is at home, building a tree house in the back-yard with his son. May I take a message?"

The receptionist's reason for the chief executive's absence from his office was somewhat intriguing. The more I thought about it, the more it dawned on me that it was an impressive demonstration of his personal success. It caused me to think about what success really is compared to how it is often defined.

As the pace of society accelerates, the definition of success becomes increasingly shallow. Time being in short supply means that the time given to reporting a person's success is limited. The focus is placed entirely on their specific achievement. The reporting gives little insight into the person behind the achievement. The result is that our minds are filled with the names of people who have been accorded the title of success which we end up believing.

Is it little wonder that we are shocked when we discover that a once impressive sports star, actor, business entrepreneur, or artist has shipwrecked their lives on the reef of self-imposed tragedy? We ask ourselves the question: "How could that happen . . . they had it all?" It is then that we realize that they did not have it all. Perhaps they had success in a singular pursuit, but this does not necessarily translate into personal success.

Our complex lives are played out on more than one field. Therefore, building a definition of success based on the achievements of one field only is misleading and undermines the meaning and significance of success. While succeeding in a singular pursuit is worthy of applause, the person who is succeeding in all fields of their life deserves a standing ovation.

Personal success cannot be assessed solely by the victories from one field of living. It is possible to have an incredible achievement in one field and live a treacherous life because that success stands in isolation. The result is a life that strains under the continual adjustments needed to be made because of the incongruity between success in one field and tragedy in others. This imbalance causes something to give way—usually personal stability. Success is meant to heighten one's enjoyment of life, not cause it to suffer. That is why success which crosses all fields of living is paramount. Not only does it bring happiness, but, it ensures that the satisfaction of succeeding lasts.

I am inspired by the chief executive who takes a day out of the office to build a tree house with his son. He exemplifies someone committed to personal success—victory in all fields of one's life.

Building a winning relationship with your desires starts by wanting success in all fields of your life, not just one.

While our lives contain many experiences, you will find that all of our experiences relate to at least one of four basic fields. All that we find impressive, all that is precious to us, all of our activities, all of our desires and hopes can be seen relating to one or more of these four fields illustrated below.

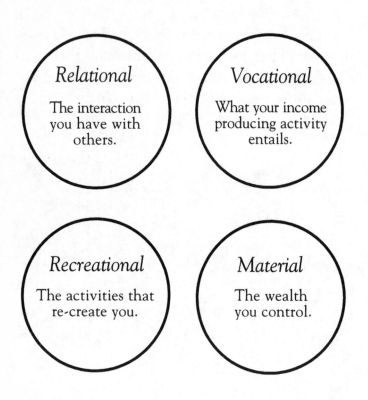

Relational

The interaction you have with others.

Vocational

What your income producing activity entails.

Recreational

The activities that re-create you.

Material

The wealth you control.

If you were asked to write a list of the things in life which you desire, you could do so with ease. Many things become the objects of our desire. All of them subtly seduce us into thinking life will be better with them rather than without them. It's not until we take the next step of considering how desires can affect the various fields of our life that we discover their value or lack of value. Some desires may indeed *add* to our lives. Some may *detract* by making our lives unbalanced.

Sorting through our desires individually and determining their influence upon each field of our life is how we determine whether the desires are good or bad. It is also the key to extracting the power from a desire—power that enables us to bring the desire into reality.

Whatever the object of the desire that you believe will elevate your life, the most important thing is to assess how it relates to the four fields of your life. This assessment commences the sorting of your desires. Putting your desires through this refinement process is where you start to distill the power from within the desire.

We've all entertained the thought: "I wish I had that." The reality is that, usually, we take it no further. The desire is contemplated in a wishful way and then tossed into the vast sea of our mind to swim around aimlessly. Unfortunately, this limits the potential of being energized by the desire. We must take the next step.

Think about the field of your life to which this desire relates. Does it include 'spin-off' benefits to other fields of your life as well? If it does, then you have started to unlock the desire's innate power to elevate your life.

The following diagram of the four fields shows some common areas of life to which our desires relate. Consider your desires as you browse this list. In the following pages, you will have the opportunity to start to align your desires with the relevant fields.

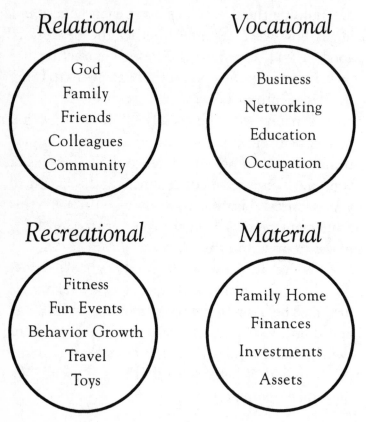

Relational

God
Family
Friends
Colleagues
Community

Vocational

Business
Networking
Education
Occupation

Recreational

Fitness
Fun Events
Behavior Growth
Travel
Toys

Material

Family Home
Finances
Investments
Assets

Several years ago, I was part of a national basketball team that toured South East Asia. We played forty games on a thirty-day tour. At the beginning of the tour we knew the toughest game was going to be against the United States Clark Air Force Base, located in the Philippines. The reality was that nobody expected us to win.

It was about the fifteenth day of the tour when we arrived at the Air Force Base. We unloaded ourselves into the basketball stadium and at that moment decided we couldn't win. Their smallest player was the size of our tallest. To make matters worse, the Air Force players extended the warm-up time so they could further display every team member's ability to do a reverse double-handed-slam dunk with a half twist. Suffice to say, we were suitably intimidated.

Our team's pre-game discussion did not revolve around a strategy for winning. Winning was out of the question. We were more concerned with how we could clutch a respectable defeat from the jaws of a humiliating pulverization.

Glen Miller, our player coach, called us together prior to the start of the game. His words were simple: "Guys, winning against this team will take a miracle, but we *can* produce that miracle if we play as a team." Apart from losing the game, our reputation, and our self-esteem, we had nothing else to lose! So we played according to Glen's advice. The advice was good—the miracle happened.

We left that stadium realizing that it wasn't our individual ability that had won the game, but how we made our individual abilities interface with each other on the court. The Clark Air Force team had as many players on the court as we had. The truth be told, regardless of the outcome, they were still better players than we were. There was a winning difference, however, between the two teams on this night. One team was made up of outstanding individuals while the other had individuals that made up an outstanding team. I'm not sure what surprised us more, winning the game or discovering the power of teamwork.

The vital principle of *teamwork* applies just as much to our desires as to sports. Our desires should not be viewed in isolation. When selecting what desires we should satisfy, we need to determine not only what they can add to one field of our life, but also what they can add to the other fields of our life. The worthy desires are the desires which have 'team-like' characteristics—the ability to positively interface with the other dimensions of one's life. These desires are best because they cause overall growth. This type of growth inevitably leads to lasting and satisfying personal success.

Significant desires will always relate to more than one field. And herein lies the key. As the number of fields to which your desire positively relates increases, so does the likelihood of the desire becoming reality. The power behind a desire that benefits one field will not be as strong as the power behind a desire that benefits two fields. Likewise, the power behind a desire that benefits two fields is not as strong as the power behind a desire that benefits three fields. Ultimately, a desire that benefits all four fields holds the most motivating power.

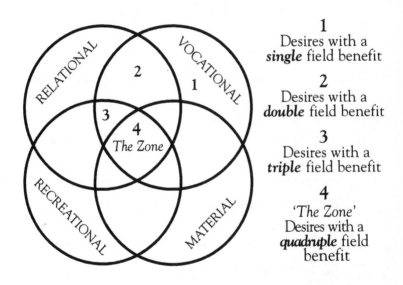

1
Desires with a
single field benefit

2
Desires with a
double field benefit

3
Desires with a
triple field benefit

4
'The Zone'
Desires with a
quadruple field
benefit

The position of quadruple overlap involves all four fields. It is a position which benefits from the motivational energy of all four fields, and results in returning benefits back to those fields. Desires that are in this special position increase the significance of one's success when they become reality.

Conversely, the same is true. The fewer fields your desire positively effects, the less significant the satisfaction of success will be in your life. In fact, as already indicated, outstanding success in one dimension of your life will only serve to highlight the emptiness of other dimensions that do not share in that success.

A dream that holds the most potential for coming true is the dream which rests in the area of quadruple overlap. I call this area of quadruple overlap 'the zone.' It's a term I have borrowed from the music world. If you ever get together with musicians, you'll hear them talk about playing 'in the zone.' It's that wonderful experience when everything clicks together and magic seems to fill the air. It's the point where all the players are in perfect unison, the sound is tight, the energy is undeniable, the audience feels it and is responding with wild enthusiasm. It's the encounter of all things coming together in a way that electrifies the atmosphere. It's an occurrence that can be dreamed about, hoped for, prepared for and one thing is for sure, when you're in the zone—you know it!

A successful life is realized when all the fields are being developed and are experiencing uplift. It is a life where the fulfillment of each dream distributes benefits to each field. In building a good relationship with your desires, you must shape them to the point where they fit into the zone. Take your mental hammer out and absolutely pound on your desire until you can see it benefiting every field of your life. A noble desire will always fit . . . so hone it and zone it!

Unlimited Attractions

Contrary to the picture of the world that the news-media paints, there is much more beauty in the world than ugliness. Far more. So much more in fact that it's common knowledge and therefore not very newsworthy. The consequence of this is that we end up hearing more about life's blunders than wonders. This is unfortunate as it conditions us to spend more time thinking about how to avoid the blunders than we do in how to soak up the wonders.

This world of wonders offers us so much. There are more attractions than we could possibly desire in a life time. It is a sad fact that some people go to their graves only having experienced few of the 'Gardens of Edens' available to them. Others scrape through life only desiring survival—this is equally sad. It is sad because it doesn't need to be this way.

Our legs are designed to run along beaches and climb up mountains. Our faces are designed to smile in response to happiness. Our eyes are designed to take in the vivid colors of grand canyons. Upon our tongues are the taste buds designed to extract the succulence from life-giving cuisine. Fingers are designed to pluck the musical strings of life. Our abdomen is designed to dance when we laugh. Our skin is designed to feel the touch of love. Our minds are designed with the capacity to experience peace and fulfillment. Our arms are designed to reach out and hold that which is beautiful. True, life is difficult, but a desire for a better life is what puts us on the pathway toward a less difficult life.

Getting on the pathway is one thing, and you know this, but staying on it is another. Your relationship with your desire is the key to staying on that pathway. You will be more able to stay on the pathway if your desire is in the zone. Sort through your desires and discard the ones that have benefit to one field of your life only. At the conclusion of this chapter there is an exercise that will help you to begin this sorting process.

The most powerful and valuable desires are gauged by how they relate to the four fields of your life. If they relate well to all fields, then you have a desire with which you can build a strong relationship. A desire that interfaces in a beneficial way with all the fields of your life, is a desire with more surfaces onto which your commitment can bond.

How One Desire Can Make Two Dreams Come True

Another great aspect about desires that have positive influence on all four fields of life, is the ability for one desire to benefit another desire. This interaction creates a magnified end result. This is called 'synergy power.'

A synergy is the phenomenon where properties work together causing the whole to be greater than the sum of the parts. This results in a greater event than what could be calculated as possible by simply adding up the benefits of the individual properties. When desires can bring a benefit across the fields of your life, it opens up the likelihood of success-producing synergies to occur.

The experience of a friend of mine named Steve is a fine example of this. He was in his final year of technical training to become a home builder. The desire to start his own business fueled his dream of one day being a home builder of fine repute. He knew it was a competitive vocation as there were plenty of building companies to service the new housing demand. At the same time, Steve was coming to grips with a growing desire to provide his wife and children with a home they could call their own.

When Steve was a teenager, his father bought a block of land which he gave to Steve. The land was purchased at a 'give-away' price. The reason for this was that the land was very steep in gradient, averaging a 45° degree slope from top to bottom. Few people had built on the surrounding area as the civil engineering costs in creating a level place for the house foundations and concrete slab were exorbitant.

Steve recognized this and decided it was better for him to sell the land for whatever he could get for it and use the proceeds as a deposit on an existing house. Two obstacles stood in his way of proceeding with this plan. First, because of the difficulties involved in building on such a gradient, no one was interested in buying the land. Second, even if a buyer was found, the proceeds from the sale would not be sufficient for a deposit on a house which would meet their needs.

In spending time with Steve, he related to me his dilemma. Having seen the land, I knew that the most probable buyer would be a builder who could devise a way of building on it without incurring the costs that a conventional home design would cause. So I threw Steve the challenge: "You're a builder— if you can devise a way to build on your land, there would be two major benefits in doing so.

First, you would not have to wait for a buyer who may not materialize for months, or maybe even years. Secondly, you own a clear title on the land. Any funds you put together could go straight into building materials and what's more, you could purchase those materials cheaper than most people because of your status as a tradesman. All you need to do is come up with a different way to arrive at the same end: the goal of getting a house on your land."

Steve did come up with a viable design. It involved the employment of a largely under-utilized form of building called 'pole frame construction.' As there were no builders specializing in that type of construction, Steve was on his own to work out the unique challenges. Engineering the foundation alone called for twenty-five timber poles, some over thirty feet tall, standing vertically out of the ground on top of which the floor was built. As the house took shape, so did Steve's dreams for starting his building company.

Now, years later, Steve is the managing director of his own construction company that employs many people and specializes in building pole frame homes. Having built more homes this way than any other builder in the region, he has an acclaimed reputation. He also has the pride of knowing that his intense desire to provide a home for his family synergized with his desire to become a renowned builder. Steve's success in one field has spilled into success in the other fields of his life.

Good Dreams Don't Drown You

In sorting through the desires which you find attractive, you must keep in mind that there is one thing worse than not having a dream, and that is having a dream which drowns you. The precious benefit in building a good relationship with a desire is that it requires you to contemplate what effects the desire can have on your whole life, not just part of it. It's resolving how your dream can build and develop your life, not drown it. Resolving this brings validity to the pursuit of your dream.

You may have heard many times that in order to succeed you have to 'give it 100% commitment.' There is truth in this, however, in view of the complete picture of our lives it can be a misleading concept. Too many times, I come across people so intensely bent on 'making it' that they live a torrid life of anxiety in the process. They seem to shelve the need for joy in life while they navigate the meteoroids, with the intention of taking joy back off the shelf as their reward for having reached the moon. Those who have experienced this type of existence will be the first to tell you that if you can't be happy along the way—reaching the goal will not give you lasting happiness.

I recently received a letter from a man who went to great lengths to tell me of all the motivational books he had read, and how unhappy he was at not attaining what he desired. The tone of his letter was that of despair. In short, his desires had become a tyranny for him. It did not take me too long to realize that he did not have a good relationship with his desires. They were causing him more anguish than good. Clearly he was hanging all his hopes of happiness on attaining success in one field of life only.

How precarious it is to focus on one field of life at the exclusion of others. It makes a person vulnerable to instability and doesn't necessarily ensure the likelihood of achieving one's dreams. A dream well related to always leaves a person elevated, not eliminated. Personal success and personal sanity were never meant to be mutually exclusive terms.

Yes, a dream calls for our full effort. But, if we lose ourselves in the process, we aren't fulfilling a dream—we're serving an obsession. An obsession inevitably erodes personal happiness by making one's life unbalanced. The relationship you have with your desire is what determines whether it is a dream or an obsession.

If a desire in one field is causing you to neglect the other fields of your life, then it is not a desire in the zone. Truly successful people give 100% commitment to a desire only when they relate to it as something which positively impacts all fields of their life. The hallmark of someone obsessed by their desire is seen in the way it negatively affects other important fields of their life.

One of the greatest lessons I learned at the university where I was trained came from the counsel of one of my professors outside of the lecture room. Having been summoned to her office, I speculated that the lecturer's advice was going to be in relation to academic endeavors. This occasion was different. She sat me down and proceeded to advise the person in me, not the student. At first she indicated her approval of an ability that I had displayed. Then she went on to say that she was afraid that it would lead to my downfall.

This came as a shock, because in the ability of which she spoke, I thought she would be pleased at my earnest desire to become the best. Puzzled I asked, "Shouldn't I be doing all I can to develop my strengths?" "Yes," she replied, "but not at the expense of building relationships. You have the ability of turning in great performances. But, the day you turn in a dud is the day people will devour you because you haven't connected with them relationally. Yes, aim for the moon with what you're good at, but invest love in people along the way. And if, heaven forbid, you should ever turn in a dud, you won't need to worry because their love for you will help to get you back on the launching pad."

Her name was Dianne, and that ten minute meeting in her office rescued me from drowning in the perfection orientation which had come to dominate me. Three months later, while on a research assignment in Papua New Guinea, the plane in which she was a passenger lost altitude and she lost her life. Dianne practiced what she preached. She played hard, but not at the expense of moments where she built relationships. Her life was short on years but not on significance.

Honing and Zoning
Our Desires

True success does not require you to sacrifice who you are in the process. Rather, true success develops who you are in the process.

Those who become obsessed by a specific desire may still reach their goal. The difficulty is that by the time they reach it, they are so disoriented in life that they're not sure who they are. Thus comes the lament heralded by some, "I climbed to the top of my ladder and discovered I was leaning on the wrong wall!" People in this situation are not good ambassadors of success. They fail to be able to relate positively to dreams coming true. Not because the dream didn't deliver, but because their journey was detrimental. They lost sight of themselves along the way, and therefore, when they finally achieved their goal, it merely highlighted their emptiness.

Fortunately, we are never asked to lose ourselves in the process of having our dreams come true. Nor, are we asked to become obsessed. The sacrifice we are asked to make is to take a moment to put ourselves through the process of getting our desires aligned and relating positively to our whole lives. The necessary commitment, effort, and strategies are then built on that solid foundation. The result, simply put, is that the desires of our hearts will eventuate because we gave the effort to get our hearts right in the first place.

It is time for you to hone your desires so that you see them fitting in the zone. Engage yourself in the exercises on the following pages before you continue reading about the second stage of building a winning relationship with your desires.

◆

Desire Evaluation Exercise

Space is provided on the following pages to list your greatest desires in each field. See how gaining what you desire can spill over to benefit the other fields of your life. This exercise helps you gain a clear picture in your mind of how your dream relates to your whole life. If the benefits of your desires reach across all of the fields, you have painted a strong picture that will more readily stay in your mind when the challenges come.

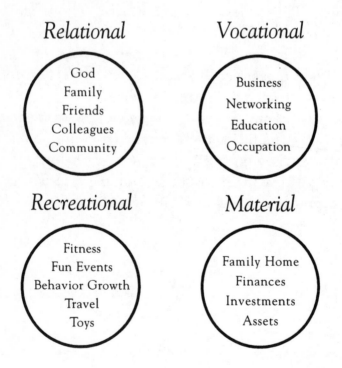

Relational

God
Family
Friends
Colleagues
Community

Vocational

Business
Networking
Education
Occupation

Recreational

Fitness
Fun Events
Behavior Growth
Travel
Toys

Material

Family Home
Finances
Investments
Assets

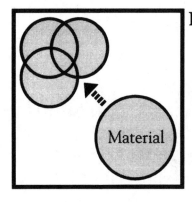 **Date:** _____

Material Desires
EVALUATION

My material desire is

_____

Gaining this desire benefits me:

Vocationally by

_____

_____

Relationally by

_____

_____

Recreationally by

_____

_____

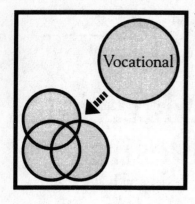

Date:

_____

Vocational
Desires
EVALUATION

My vocational desire is

_____

Gaining this desire benefits me:

Relationally by

_____

_____

Materially by

_____

_____

Recreationally by

_____

_____

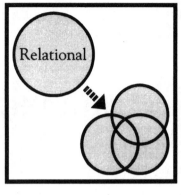

Date: _____

Relational Desires
EVALUATION

My relational desire is

_____

Gaining this desire benefits me:

Recreationally by

_____

_____

Vocationally by

_____

_____

Materially by

_____

_____

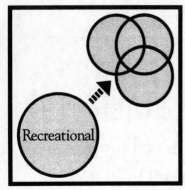

Date: _____

Recreational
Desires
EVALUATION

My recreational desire is

_____

Gaining this desire benefits me:

Materially by

_____

_____

Relationally by

_____

_____

Vocationally by

_____

_____

Stage 2

Making the Right Choice
(Found What I've Been Looking For)

◆

> *Great people desire things that will help other people, not hurt them.*

WE ARE BORN TO DESIRE. It may even be the strongest force within us. We can't deny its power. We can't even avoid it. But we can direct it where we choose. As a force, it is neutral. It is the attitude behind the desire that determines whether it leads to constructive or destructive ends.

When you look at it honestly, there are some things we can desire that involve sabotaging the

37

well being of others. This being the case, some people still proceed, but not without sabotaging a part of themselves in the process. Integrity demands that we not gain what we want at the expense of others. The good news is that the greatest desires do not lead us to hurting people but rather helping them.

Guilt-free Desire

While desire is basically a selfish thing, that doesn't necessarily mean it's a bad thing nor something about which we should feel guilty. True, selfish desires that have a negative effect on ourselves or others need to be called seriously into question. But just as true is the fact that our personal desires can bring good things into the lives of others. Therefore, though desires can start at a selfish level, they do not need to remain there. The greatest personal desires are the ones that incorporate others and result in benefiting them. In developing a good relationship with your desires, direct your desires toward nobility.

I once heard someone say, "You have more potential for achieving your dream if it benefits the ones you care for rather than if it only benefits yourself." In the face of challenge, a goal that only benefits oneself is more readily given up on, than a goal that benefits the ones we care for.

Don't be fooled. Living is not a case of 'will I or won't I?' have desires. You *will* have them, regardless of who you are, and you will give in to them eventually, whether you are a dream achiever or not. You might as well make your desires noble and harness the innate power of desire to be useful in making life greater for everyone.

There is a saying: "You'll never do the right thing if it is born out of a wrong motive." Your desires, however, can be firmly based in magnificent motives. The coming true of any dream that was motivated by a desire to benefit all concerned credits the dreamer as noble. Suppressing desire is never the answer. Primarily, we must examine the desire and measure its value on the scale of the effect the desire will have on everybody. Then, steer the desire in the direction where it will have the most profound positive effect.

There is no benefit in pruning our potential under the guise that by denying our desires, we attain some sanctimonious level of civic mindfulness. The most inspirational people I know are the ones who, rather than denying their desires, take charge of them, tailoring them to be helpful in achieving great things. 'Guilt free' desire is good. It is not so much what you lay your eyes upon that is good or bad. It is not so much what you want that is good or bad. It is what these things do to you that determines their value.

A good relationship can be judged by what you become in that relationship. That is why positively geared people should avoid the courts of negative people. To enter a negative domain establishes a oneness in relationship with it. This type of relationship increases the likelihood that you will begin to reflect the nuances of this domain.

Transfer this reasoning to your relationship with your desires. If your desire brings out the best in you, then you are well on the way to having a healthy relationship with what you want.

A healthy relationship with one's desire is what paves the way for the desire to turn into a dream. A dream, therefore, is a desire that has a mature reason for being in one's life, the reason being that the desire is helping to bring out your best qualities.

Puppy Love

I remember the first time someone applied this term to me. It was the mid-nineteen-seventies. I was in my early teens and a particular night at a youth function put me in a trance for days. Something took place in the parking lot after the socializing had drawn to a close. Two sisters from another youth group had, for the past few weeks, taken the journey across town to join with our group. Needless to say, they were given the royal welcome by the guys in our group who would become a little goofy every time they showed up. These sisters were one of God's lessons to young guys on physiology—how visual stimuli can increase pulse rate and blood pressure.

For some reason, I ended up walking with these girls to the parking lot. The one who was driving made her way around the other side of the car. As I cheerfully said goodbye, the other one came up and planted a kiss that made me melt into a beautiful world. It was totally unexpected and completely acceptable! I floated through the next days, my mind rarely digressing from that heavenly experience. The moment was meticulously replayed in my mind in slow motion and complete with frame by frame action replay analysis. I'm sure my

41

mental video player wore out. This was true love and without doubt I was indeed looking forward to it flourishing into full relational bloom.

About twelve days later, after realizing that the relational fire set ablaze by a kiss was actually in danger of dying (no phone calls, no letters, no contact), I summoned the courage to talk to a mutual friend. It was then that I discovered that the girl was three years ahead of me in high school, already had a boyfriend, and was just compelled in a moment of magical fellowship to show some affection. "In short, Wes," the mutual friend said, "it's puppy love. . . don't worry, you'll get over it!"

Disappointment was only the beginning. How could something so real to me be so quickly written off as puppy love? Then someone explained to me that is why it's called puppy love— because it is real in the eyes of the puppy.

A person excited by a new dream is an easy target for the same 'level headed' sentiment—"It's only real in your eyes. . . don't worry you'll soon get over it!"

This is one of the significant challenges that a person with a dream experiences. When you tell someone about your dream, there is no guarantee that the idea will be received in a positively affirming way. Though what we share may be seriously real to us, we can be criticized as "not having our feet grounded in reality." They may not say it to our face, but they sure send the signals. Maybe that's why we are conditioned as we grow up to keep our dreams to ourselves. Too many people have written off our desires as 'puppy love', some even going so far as to say "don't worry you'll get over it." If their pessimism isn't serious enough, our mind seems to have a 'built-in' default switch which draws our attention to the memory of their pessimism every time we stumble in the early stage of a challenge.

There is always the chance that others will view your dream as silly. But, if the dream is real for you, then that is all that matters for the moment. You are beginning a relationship with something that has the potential to elevate your life forever. Time and experience may shape the relationship with your desire, but isn't that to be expected with any relationship?

The personal development you will experience through embarking on a relationship with a noble desire will do more for you than all the well-intended pessimism you will ever encounter. At the end of the day, people's skepticism, no matter how well-intentioned, will do nothing to transport you in the direction of improvement.

While reflecting on the inevitability of those who think your dreams are silly, I'm *not* advocating keeping your dreams locked away in the vault of your heart, safe from the view of all others. There is sizeable value in letting others know where you are specifically heading. Some days when you're weary, the knowledge that there are spectators checking on your score will be all the motivation you have. If you are intent to manicure a reputation for results, it's good to let people know that you have committed yourself to the game.

Be prepared, however, for some to think you are infatuated with something they believe can not materialize. Regardless of what they think, do not be short-circuited by these people, especially if they haven't done anything significant with their life. In fact, these people are generally the ones who specialize in handing out pearls of mud.

You've Got That Loving Feeling

You would not marry a person you would be ashamed to be seen with, would you? So, a rule in building a good relationship with your desires is to commit yourself to desires with which you are proud to associate.

Once you've clarified this in your mind, you start to develop the relationship by seeing where it takes you. If your dream is starting to enthuse you, then you've chosen wisely. If, when contemplating your desire, you find yourself musing of ways to make the desire become real, then you know you have gripped something which is motivating you. The power of desire is starting to work for you. Furthermore, because it is a desire you are proud to have association with, you are building something which will rescue you in days to come—a good relationship.

Ask yourself: If my dream came true would I be excited enough to tell everybody about it? If you can say yes to this, then quit being timid and uncommitted. Take another look at how your desire fits into the zone and become empowered by that knowledge. Then, get on with the relationship building.

You Light Up My Life

I have seen people spring back to life when they connected with something which gave them reason to consider the future bright and possible. Conversely, I have seen people literally pass away because they had no reason to look forward to the future. There is nothing more debilitating to a person's enthusiasm than when they see no possibility of experiencing joy in their coming days. The right choice of desire, however, has a way of bringing hope into one's existence. Hope envelopes more motivational power than all other words in language save two (faith and love. . . which are connected to hope anyway). Making the right choice in what you want in life helps eradicate the gloominess that typifies a life with no purpose.

Hope is the light that all the darkness in the world can't put out. Life does not exist where there is no hope. Without it, we are dead. Oh, we may still breathe, eat, move around, but even though it may take them another forty years until they can bury us, without hope we are not living.

There are people who just hope to get through the day. While for some in traumatic situations this is a considerable exercise of the power of hope, for the rest of us, this is not hope. It is merely wanting the obvious. Real hope gives us unparalleled energy to tackle big challenges. It infuses us with the will to move forward. It unleashes power to help us carry on when it seems useless to do so. Real hope releases an aura of inspiration, the glow of which other people can see.

A mighty desire, a great dream, is a basis for hope. If the ones you care for, if your community, if your society, if your nation stands in need of anyone—it would not be another critic or judge or realist—it stands in need of a human radiating with the rays of optimism about the future. A person like you. You, whose hope of heart and desire for a grand destiny will serve to propel you into success. And, in doing so, help others realize that life can be better if they desire it to be.

Elevation out of the quicksand of a directionless life of unrealized potential happens when you consider the future as the platform for the fulfillment of your desires. Your aspirations actually rescue you. I am grateful for having been rescued many times. To know this and to remind myself of this, broadens the base of appreciation for my desires. I often ask myself, "Where would I be now if I didn't have them?"

The place of desire can be profoundly appreciated for how it illuminates your view of the future. Don't forget this. There will be times when you will want to curse your desires because they lead you through the dark valleys of challenge. But without them, you would have had no reason to take the journey at all.

You're The One That I Want

It was a beautiful afternoon on New Year's Day and Eleanor and I had decided to wander around the city shopping mall together. Walking into a men's clothing store, I was approached by a shop assistant offering his help. I was looking for a shirt that I could wear for work so he immediately ushered me over to the business shirt section. Explaining to him that wasn't the type of work shirt I was looking for, I picked up a glitzy gold silk shirt and said, "This is more like it!"

Puzzled, he enquired as to what type of work would cause me to need a shirt like that. The more I told him, the more he became inquisitive at the notion of a living that was made through performing on stage and writing for the same. He let slip a few remarks to the tune of 'it must be nice to consider that your work.' The store was deserted, except for us and given that his response harbored a tone of discontent, I decided to spend a few moments sowing some encouragement into his life.

I engaged him in a conversation about his job at the store then I asked him what he would rather be doing for a living. He said, "Riding jet skis and chasing my girlfriend around the world." I said, "Well, I'm not sure there's anyone out there willing to pay you to do that." He laughed and agreed. Then I said, "With your talent and enthusiasm you could be doing a whole lot better than what you're doing in this place, couldn't you?" He responded, "I don't know, I'm doing all right for someone my age." This confused me, for just moments before he had been telling me that his desires did not include having to work on a public holiday.

The issue was not "how he was doing compared to others his age"; the issue was how was he doing compared to his capacity and dreams. Regardless, he had missed the whole point of what I was endeavoring for him to see. Why get trapped into doing something that under-utilizes your abilities and isn't what you want to be doing with your life?

There is a lever available that, when utilized, can pry a person out of such a predicament. The lever is called desire. It is a friend to those trapped. It is a friend to those bored. It is a friend to those under-utilized. It is a friend to those with loved ones.

When you love someone and you can see your desires benefiting them, you can do extraordinary things in the face of intimidating challenges. I read recently how one man was spurred on in his dream to become a successful farmer, simply by seeing how the woman he loved would benefit by his dream coming true. Alexander Crawford emigrated to Australia from Belfast in 1880. There he met Lillie

Matthews, and they fell in love. While Alexander established himself on a farm in the rough desert of the Australian outback, he wrote often to his 'Darling Lillie.' Here is one of those letters:

13 April 1882

My Dear Lillie,

. . . I do hope I will be successful on this farm. The last manager lost nearly £1,000 a year on it but everyone says it was through bad management. When I come to think of it, it seems a risky undertaking for one with so little experience as myself to undertake to manage and bring a farm, in a state of utter disorder, into good order. I have scarcely had one year's experience but if close attention to it and hard work will do anything toward making it pay, it shall not be lacking on my part.

And I am more encouraged when I think it is not myself alone I am working for but for the dearest girl living. Oh, Lillie, my own true love, I would undergo anything for your sweet sake and count it but pleasure if I but brought you the nearer to me. I often think what would life be to me now without the love of my Lillie. I managed to get along in a kind of way before but now it would be misery indeed.

'Tis the sweetest thought I have that before long I hope to take you to myself for better, there will be no

worse in it. Sure there won't. Do tell me more about yourself in your letters. Fill them up about Lillie, commence with Lillie, end with Lillie and fill the space between with the same subject, and you may add a postscript about her, too, and it will not be too much. It is a subject I never weary reading about, writing about, or speaking about. . .

Five long years later, Alexander and Lillie were married. The power of desire not only brought them together but it helped Alexander conquer the harsh conditions to become a successful farmer.

What is the one thing you really want? Have you considered the beneficial effect it can have on you in all fields of your life?

Take a few moments and picture yourself experiencing the beneficial effect of your desire becoming reality.

Now take a few moments to consider how many lives you will help because your dream came true. Picture their excitement when you pass the goodness on to them. Imagine the pride you'll feel to have achieved. Picture how proud others will be of you.

Have you pictured it completely in your mind? Have you mentally stood before your desire and declared to yourself, "Yes, this is truly what I want!"?

If you can say yes, then you have discovered what you want and have started to build a good relationship with what you want. You can say, "I am good friends with my desire because when I relate to it, I like what it does to me—I like who I become."

Now for Stage Three . . .

◆

Stage 3

Finding Out the Cost

(The 'Getting to Know You' Phase)

◆

> *Bonding with your dream involves accepting the dream's price because you appreciate its value.*

T HE MORTALITY RATE FOR DREAMS is higher during this stage than any other. It happens this way. Being all pumped up with excitement for a dream, a person starts the research process. What is it going to take? How far am I short? What is the cost? They reach for the price tag and discover that it costs more than what they have to spend. Much more. Their mental calculations lead them to the wrenching discovery that to make up the short fall, more effort is required than first imagined. Then the arguments start. The arguments between the respective desires—the desire for the dream and the desire for continued comfort. The fighting breaks out. Back and forth the desires will joust in one's mind until one delivers a fatal blow to the other. One desire emerges the victor; the other is slain. Which desire is more likely to win? The desire for the dream or the desire for continued comfort? The answer: *the desire that is fed the most is the one that will triumph*.

Take Your Desire Out To Dinner

While the excitement we have about our newly discovered dream is compelling, it's not enough to build the strength of relationship one needs with the desire to make it come true. Excitement is a great feeling to have, but its limitations need to be acknowledged. It can diminish as quickly as it came. It's certainly not a strong enough base upon which to build a lasting relationship. Do not think that the excitement for a dream is all you need to make the dream become reality. It is one step in the process, and though an important step, it is a frail one all the same.

The important facet of excitement is in its ability to motivate us to find out more. When we seek to find out more, our reward comes in the form of vital information. Information that helps us better calculate the impact of the dream in relation to our life. It means that intellect and reason add their weight to strengthen our relationship with the dream. We're able to imagine ourselves existing in the realm of the dreamed future with more clarity. If the facts measure up to what our imagination of the facts are, then there is a greater basis for commitment.

The idea of owning a new car, for example, may be where your dream starts. A frustrating breakdown in your current worn out vehicle may have given rise to the dream. You realize that a new car is what you'd like. A few days later you notice a friend drive past in a brand new car. The dream stirs within you as you notice how sharp the shiny new car makes your friend look. Your desire to have the same sets up a subconscious radar system in your mind. Whether you see them advertised on television, or as you pass them on the road, you start to take greater notice of new cars. One afternoon, while walking the dog, you decide to vary your usual route to include a quick look at the local dealership where you pick up a full-color brochure of a particular model which appeals to you. That night you sit up in bed reading the brochure, all the time envisioning your life with such an acquisition and getting excited!

But that's not enough. Car dealers know it's not enough. That's why they are so eager for a prospective customer to move on to the next step of the "getting to know you phase"—taking the car for a test drive. The all-crucial touch of personal experience.

Car dealers know that up to now, your excitement for the dream is largely imagination based. They want to give you a favorable encounter of the dream so your view of the dream becomes more stimulated by personal experience than the speculation of your imagination.

If you test drive the car and it fails to live up to what you imagined, this personal experience has worked to the car dealer's disadvantage. It's a risk car dealers are willing to take, however, because of the enormous advantage a test drive can produce. When your personal experience matches or exceeds what you imagined of your dream, then the car dealer has succeeded in changing your stimulation from being imagined in the mind to experienced in reality. Your stimulation has changed from excitement towards the dream, to enthusiasm for the dream. The difference is this: in its motivational qualities, enthusiasm outlasts excitement and leads to greater commitment.

As one's positive experience and knowledge of something grows, so their commitment to it grows. Commitment is a quality by which every relationship is strengthened. Therefore, it is important to get to know all you can about your dream. If what you discover builds on your previous judgment, then your excitement for it will evolve into enthusiasm. A much stronger relationship is the end result.

Some may ask at this point, "Doesn't familiarity with the dream take some of the mystery out of it and the associated passion for its acquisition?" The answer is yes. Only the dreams that are really worth having survive this type of scrutiny. Let me illustrate this.

An adventurous friend and I were invited to go boating on a beautiful canyon lake in Southern California. On the way to joining the boat owner, my friend was musing as to whether he should buy a boat since he lived so close to the water himself. It was an idea sparked by the knowledge that the boat we were going out on was actually for sale. In the thrilling moments of entertainment that the speed boat provided, I thought my friend was well bitten by the boating bug. He said in the heat of the excitement, "Yeah, I'd love to own a boat." My friend has just become a boat owner, I thought. I was wrong.

Later that night, he admitted that while the boating excursion was enjoyable, it was not enough to compel him to proceed with the notion of owning a boat. In essence, the personal experience had failed to turn his excitement for the idea into enthusiasm for the idea.

If a test drive encounter doesn't heighten your desire, that's terrific. The test drive has helped you realize your affections were misplaced. Admit it, dismantle your attraction, and get on with finding something that does survive the test drive. When you find something that does, you uncover the energy to help you to reach what you are aiming for. Personal experience transforms the nature of your motivation from excitement to a far stronger and lasting enthusiasm.

There are people you will come across who will be skeptical about this whole 'pursuing a dream' concept. They are skeptical for one of two reasons; either they have never pursued a dream, or they have pursued a dream and, upon achieving it, realized that it wasn't what they wanted after all. If people of the latter scenario involved themselves in the important 'getting to know you' stage, they would have no cause to be skeptical.

This stage gives the opportunity for one to work out early in the journey whether the fulfillment of the dream is really what they want. To not take the opportunity of getting to know your dream is as foolish as committing yourself to a marriage before getting to know your prospective partner.

Years ago, I toyed with the notion of adding another dimension to my profession by way of a law qualification. The more I contemplated the idea and imagined myself in a courtroom situation, the more my excitement grew. I decided that the notion was worthy of endeavor. My next step was to enroll in a law course being taught at Sydney University.

After four months, and after having completed a series of major assignments, I began to re-evaluate whether it was what I really wanted to do. The relationship with my dream was suffering at the hands of gained knowledge. It became evident that the cost involved was overshadowing my desire to proceed.

No, it wasn't the cost of effort, time, or finances. I was quite willing to pay those costs. It seemed from my perspective that the life of a lawyer was looking more like a life of being involved in fights between adults. For me, this was a price too high. It was not a desirable way to spend the moments of my life.

Now, before those in the law profession take offense, the point I am making is this: If my desire to be a lawyer was strong enough, it would have survived regardless of what my personal experience in the arena of law caused me to discover. Taking the law profession for a 'test drive' helped me to realize that my character and temperament would not have been fully appreciated nor utilized in that world.

I am glad I took that dream out to dinner a few times. It helped me to discover that there was not enough relationship with the dream to warrant me proposing marriage to it!

A Dream Worth Losing Sleep Over

If the dream passes the scrutiny of the 'getting to know you' phase, then it is a dream that will survive as long as you survive. In fact, your dream will help you to survive. You go to bed not only happy about your relationship with the object of your desire, but you have a fire of enthusiasm that burns within you that will often keep you awake thinking about it.

When I was dating Eleanor, I would gladly lose hours of sleep for just a few minutes with her. One frosty morning, I arose at 4AM to commit an act of romance that I was sure would pay big dividends! We lived about an hour away from each other. Jumping on my trusty motorcycle I set off toward her house with a single red flower stuffed down my jacket. My plan was to place the flower with a heartfelt note on her doorstep and leave. Riding away from her home, the plan in effect, I imagined the outcome. Eleanor would rush out the door on her way to college and be met with this beautiful flower to help her start her day.

That night I received a phone call as anticipated. The plan didn't exactly work as I'd hoped. Eleanor's sister ran out the door first, not seeing the flower, crushed it into the doormat. It didn't matter. It was still a pleasure to lose sleep for the sake of someone about whom I dreamed.

If the dream is compelling enough for you to lose sleep over, be assured you have a relationship forming that will outlast the crushing of a thousand flowers.

Don't Reach For The Price Tag First

It's fun to be sitting around a table in conversation with the parents of young children. Getting on to the subject of babies brings to the conversation all manner of horror stories; from the baby's ability to eject milk onto the left shoulder of every nice outfit you own; to the stark reality that the onset of parenthood is like being given a gift of a 'pre-set' early morning alarm clock with no snooze button. The conversation is invariably punctuated with much laughter, empathetic groans and statements like "I remember the time when. . ."

It would be understandable if an outsider left the conversation thinking anyone would have to be crazy to want to have children. Then, when everyone has exhausted their repertoire of gross stories, someone will offer the closing remark, "Yeah, but becoming a father/mother is the best thing that ever happened to me. . . I could not imagine life without my kids." Somehow, we are more able to express the downsides of parenthood easier than the upsides—even though the positives far outweigh the negatives.

It can work the same way when discovering

the cost of our dreams. The tendency to ponder the negatives first is tempting. I don't know if you're like me, but when I stand in front of something desirable, my first impulse is to reach for the price tag. Many times this throws a bucket of iced water over the desire before it has a chance to fully heat my senses. In recent years, I have discovered it's much better to get to know the qualities so that I can appreciate the reasons for the cost. Sure it's important to find out the cost. Knowing the cost is integral to getting to know your dream. But don't reach for the price tag first. Give the fire a chance to get started. In doing so, you are familiarizing yourself with the features and benefits of your desire before you subject it to the impact of a bucket of cold water.

Remember it's what the dream costs you which makes the dream worth the price. *Expect* to be overawed by the cost. If you are not, then what you have set your eyes upon is an easy target. Achievement that comes easily, comes at the expense of not being able to appreciate it.

Train yourself to respond positively to being shocked at the cost. Instead of viewing the cost as a declaration of how far you are currently short of the mark, view it as a certificate of how much you will value it when your efforts gain its reward.

Next time you hear someone say "it's not worth the price," ask yourself whether the response is related to their having had personal experience of its features and benefits, or whether they are just trying to justify their position of being so far short of acquiring what they see as costing so much.

When you build a good relationship with your dream, you see the cost of the dream not as the 'hidden' downside, but as one of its valuable benefits.

Going To The Movies

Having achieved something significantly monumental in my life, I am sometimes asked the question: "How did it feel when it happened?" My answer is always in the order of, "Great. . . terrific". However, if I was to be more accurate I would say, "It felt right!" For the reality is the achievement was experienced in my mind long before it was achieved physically. In a way, you could say that I fully expected it to happen so that when it finally did, I wasn't surprised.

I heard a marriage counselor say recently that people in troubled marriages walk out on their spouses psychologically long before they ever do physically. She went on to say that leaving psychologically helped the process of leaving physically eventuate. My counselling involvement in people's lives over the years bears testimony to this being true. My experience has shown how the principle also works for positive ends. By arriving somewhere psychologically first, the process of eventually arriving there physically is helped.

Remind yourself of the saying: **Reality rises to what the mind devises.** Accompanying your dream in a mental movie is one of the most powerful ways to program your mind.

Dream Weaving

Experiencing your dream in a mental movie not only helps you get to know your dream, to build expectation and set your direction, it also gives you the opportunity to anticipate the changes success will bring. It helps you to weave the pieces together before they are all thrown into your lap. In effect, you are putting yourself through a rehearsal. This is important preparation.

When your dream comes true, change is inevitable. To contemplate the changes ahead of time gives you the chance to thoughtfully consider how you will respond to the changes. Your feelings, your attitudes, your expectations, your inclinations will all be under the fire of the 'heat of the moment'. It is an exciting and mentally intoxicating time, but also a time when you can make some stupid mistakes. Mistakes that can be easily avoided if you think about the experience before hand.

You are more likely to adjust favorably to the exciting 'heady' heat of success, if in your mind, you have woven the pieces together to form a strategy on how you will respond to the success when it comes.

I remember hearing the world-famous singer and songwriter, Sting, being interviewed on his thoughts regarding a particular development in the music industry. Well-positioned music producers were selecting young television stars and with the help of their finely tuned music manufacturing and marketing processes, turning these kids into pop icons overnight. In recalling his own rise to stardom, Sting said that it was years of having to lug his back-breaking equipment up and down the stairs of obscure hotels that strengthened him to be able to cope with the pressure of success when it finally came. When he achieved success, Sting was prepared and has more than coped—he has gone on from strength to strength.

On the other hand, the young television stars were breaking under the pressure of the rapid change their success was bringing. They had not built a mental foundation capable of holding them up during their time of adjusting to a new level of existence.

Friends of mine tell the story of their experience in responding to achieving great success financially. After years of hard work, the financial dam relaxed and the dollars started flowing in at a very rapid rate. They did what seemed a perfectly acceptable thing to do. They started spending! A little while later, with much consternation, they had to financially reorganize themselves in a hurry at the insistence of the I.R.S. wanting their share.

Continually reminding yourself that to get what you want involves more than ordinary effort is fundamental to succeeding. To **achieve** great success you need to demonstrate a working knowledge of all the fundamental principles of success. To **enjoy** great success depends on having built a good relationship with your desire.

Building a good relationship with your desire involves facing up to the cost of getting what you want but also realizing that there will still be some costs once you *have* what you want.

If your desire is noble, knowledge of this will not dampen your drive, but instead mature your drive. Success will inevitably bring some challenges, but your good relationship with your desire will empower you to move forward without faltering in your progress.

◆

Investing in the Dream
(Picking Up the Tab)

◆

> *That which receives some of your treasure,*
> *receives some of your heart.*

AS A YOUNG GUY, when I discovered a girl that I liked a lot, I would seek to find out all I could about that girl. You would find me asking questions of people who knew her, such as, "What do you know about Jane? What is she like?" Third parties could tell me a certain amount about her, but to get any closer, I had to come in from afar and introduce myself. In other words, I had to physically reach out to her in a bid to develop the relationship. It would call for an investment of my time which would inevitably lead to an investment of some financial resources in the dating process.

Investing your money in a relationship, signals that you are serious. It's your tangible demonstration of enthusiasm for developing the relationship.

So it goes with our dreams. Having discovered as much as we can about what we want and how much it will cost, then comes the next step—the investment of our resources into what we want. It is an essential step in building the desired alliance. This does not mean we're *committed*. But rather, we are *committing*, through our wallet, more of our heart to the dream.

Wooing The Dream With Your Wallet

If one's connection with his or her dream costs only emotional and mental energy plus a bit of time, then the dream remains extremely vulnerable. In the face of challenge, a dream that has not cost you anything from the hip pocket or the purse can easily be discarded. Further strengthening of one's commitment to a dream requires action, specifically, financial investment action. In other words: *Put some money into your dream!*

Investing money into your dream is the first clear signal of the relationship. This investment is not primarily a signal for the world's benefit, rather it's a signal for your benefit. Why is it for your benefit? Because in the early stages of relating to your dream, the greatest enemy to your dream's safety is *you*. If anyone can sabotage it, you will be the most likely offender. Investing your resources will help stem the likelihood of you committing this offense.

When you haven't invested much into your dream, you are always at risk to opt out under pressure. However, once you've laid out physical resources as a token of personal investment it takes away the capacity for one to exercise the easy 'I've changed my mind' option.

To a degree, investing in your dream is like paying a non-refundable deposit. It motivates you to pursue the call of your dream rather than be seduced by the soft option of 'chickening out'. It encourages you to stay with your dreams, even when your feelings are telling you otherwise.

For years I dreamed of writing a book. And for years, there it stayed. . . in my mind. Then one day, the evidence of this dream manifested itself in something other than my mind. I spent some money on my dream. As a result, my dream became firmly registered on my bank statement. Had I been hit by a bus before that day, I would have left no physical evidence of attachment to my dream. But had I been hit by a bus after that day, three very physical, very tangible entities would have known about my dream: namely my accountant, my bank manager and finally, the I.R.S.

Let me explain. Having consulted my wife about wanting to write a book, her counsel helped me realize that I would never write it in my normal environment. There were too many distractions. The biggest distraction was myself! I was always being lured by other activities that produced more immediate gratification.

It was decided, with Eleanor's blessing, that I would set aside a month out of my performing schedule, travel to a solitary place, and get seriously down to writing. The deal was that I could go anywhere in the world to write as long as it would help me become focussed and would not serve as a distraction from the task. A non-refundable plane ticket was purchased to a remote destination, and from that day on, I was more connected with my dream than ever before. The relationship with my dream had proceeded to the point where my bank statement was declaring my intentions!

The day Eleanor took me to the airport I carried something other than a suitcase. I carried a burden of responsibility. Precious family resources had been spent in financing this trip. I felt responsible to my family and knew that I had to return 'with the goods'. If I came home empty-handed, having goofed around, I would have done my family an injustice. 'Writer's block' could not be an option. This dream had already cost resources valuable to us. The investment of funds demanded unwavering commitment to the dream coming true.

Let me state again: Investing in your dream is the non-refundable commitment of your resources, motivating you to pursue the call of your dream, rather than to be seduced by the soft option of 'chickening out.' It encourages you to carry on even when your feelings are telling you otherwise.

Some might become alarmed at this point thinking, "Hey! This is a subversive plot to trick me into sticking with a course of action about which I may later change my mind." The truth is, you will feel like changing your mind later on, and changing it back again, and changing it back again, and changing it back again, and again, and again! Our feelings have the uncanny ability to have us changing our mind like the weather. What rescues us from the peril of our feelings is the knowledge of this one fact: Quit now and I've got a lot to lose!

The test of people's commitment to their dream is seen in whether they're willing to invest their money into it. This quickly sorts out whether a person's relationship with his or her dream is just a matter of good intentions, or real intentions that are backed up with purposeful action.

There is a furniture store in our town which is in a class of its own in selling furniture of particular distinction. And they know it! Their only competition is beyond a mountain range and some considerable distance. They also have fallen prey to the privileges that come with holding a monopoly on the market. They are not, for example, under pressure from competition to perform in the shipping department. Their efficiency of supply, I discovered, frustrates customers eager to acquire their purchases.

Some time ago, my wife and I purchased some furniture there. As was expected they could not immediately supply, yet they required a substantial percentage deposit. Our total purchase was well into several thousand dollars, which meant our deposit was significant. Then the waiting started. First it was weeks, then it was months.

I remember wondering many times, as the delivery date became more elusive, whether we should give up waiting for them and start again with another store. What stopped us from doing so? The knowledge that we had already committed financial resources to the order. Had we not made a deposit, a few weeks of battling impatience would have motivated us to back out of arrangements with that store and go somewhere else, or even reconsider spending that much. The knowledge that to change direction at that point would have cost us our deposit, helped us not to give in to impatient feelings. In the long run, having made the deposit worked to our advantage. Making a personal investment up front kept us on course for getting what we wanted. . . eventually!

A Patience Producing Investment

One of the unfortunate side effects of living in an exhilarating fast-paced world is that we are required less and less to exercise the virtue of patience. Many things our parents had to patiently wait for, we gain immediately. So much to the point that we have developed shorter fuses because we're so used to getting many things without delay. Almost daily I send information to the other side of the globe without thinking, "How long will it take to get there?" As soon as I send a page of information, the party on the other end is receiving it. No longer does sending information take the months it used to just a few of generations ago.

Immediate delivery is what we all want. We prefer it to waiting. Regardless, some things ask us to exercise patience and they are well worth the wait. By making a personal investment in what we are waiting for, we are less likely to change the course of our direction merely to satisfy our lack of patience. Personal investment in the dream ultimately helps us to 'hang in there' until its arrival. In other words, we have a vested interest in remaining committed to our plan.

The larger your dream, the greater the deposit you will have to make. If your dream is grand, your commitment has to be grand. Unless the commitment is grand, the relationship between you and your desire remains under-developed. To attain the necessary level for the relationship to proceed, there must be personal cost. There is no way around it. Those who try to avoid this requirement are only cheating themselves out of the benefit that commitment by personal sacrifice brings.

If sacrificing resources now as a deposit on your dream troubles you, then, you had better lower your dream or raise your commitment. Those are the only options available to you. The good news on the other hand is that, though the deposit paid on your dream does cost you, it also becomes your badge of commitment to your dream. Any person who has worn such a badge of commitment discovers that it releases energy, thrusting them further toward their dream's fulfillment.

The Pride Earned In Paying NOW!

Making a financial investment in your dream buys ownership of the dream. Therefore, you are already sharing in an aspect of the dream becoming reality. You can be proud about that.

A few years ago, I spent a day with one of the coaches of an NBA basketball team. Having my day visited by a human trainer of his magnitude, made me eager to gain his counsel on a series of matters relating to excelling in human endeavor.

"What does it take to have a high-achieving team?" I was hoping his answer to that would help me understand why our local basketball team wasn't doing so well.

His answer was simple: "First you've got to have some talent. Then you've got to train your talent to win."

I said, "Fair enough, but what happens if you

don't have the talent to start with?"

His response was, "Then you just have to prime the pump!"

"Prime the pump?" I enquired.

"That's it," he said, "if you don't have it, you've got to import it!"

I was intrigued by this principle of importing resources to help you get started. I have since come to realize that it is an essential principle in which one needs to engage in order to get what they want.

By all means, a dream that comes true can flood you with resources. Initially however, it takes imported resources to enable your progression toward the place where it can happen. In other words, a bumper harvest is never produced by planting a portion of its own yield. A bumper crop first requires the sacrifice of other seed.

The only way to part with precious resources, and feel good about it, is to view the sacrifice as a deposit on an inevitable return of wisdom and wealth.

The story of *The Pump in the Desert* illustrates this:

A sun baked and dehydrated man is crawling through the bone dry, shifting sands of a large desert. He is about to expire when he looks off into the distance and through the arid conditions sees a water pump. It's all he can do to get there. Pulling himself up by the pump handle he notices a bottle of water beside the pump with a sign. The sign reads: "Pour the contents into the pump shaft to start water flow!"

Thinking the directions were not prudent under the circumstances, the man decides to not 'waste' the water by pouring it down the pump shaft, but to drink it instead to give him energy to pump. He does so. But having felt momentarily refreshed, he soon exhausts himself pumping a handle that was producing no water. He dies.

The Moral: The man failed to realize that the sacrifice of the bottled water down the pump shaft was to moisten a leather washer inside the vacuum chamber *causing it to swell. With the leather washer in a swelled condition, a vacuum could be created by pumping the handle, thus sucking water up from the well deep below. Thousands of bottles worth of water could have been released for his refreshment, save one—the one that was needed to be sacrificed first to start the flow.*

It's easy to sacrifice out of abundance. But the sacrifice that releases abundance has to be made initially, out of scarcity. This sacrifice hurts especially when you see your friends happily using their scarce resources for, immediate entertainment— a gratification which you have courageously decided, for the time, to deny yourself.

If it hurts to invest your scarce resources now, then be proud to be paying them. Most people haven't got the courage to believe that investing scarce resources now can lead to abundant supply later. They would much rather drink the bottle than to sacrifice it in faith of a greater return.

Be proud that it hurts, because that makes you a select member of an elite group; the group that has fun splashing in the pools of abundance because they invested during the times of scarcity.

Sometimes, when I am feeling the personal cost required is exhausting, I remind myself of this fact. If it is this painful for me, then I am already far ahead of the crowd, because most of the crowd are more content to not try than to face the challenge. A friend of mine reminds himself of this principle with the saying— "If it's too tough for you. . . then it's just right for me."

A strong relationship has in its framework pride. Pride is gained through sacrifice. If you don't believe this, just try and take away the kudos from someone's achievement that they sacrificed much for, and watch the fur fly! You'll soon understand the connection between sacrifice and the esteem of the person having made the sacrifice.

So many are inclined to consider the downside of sacrifice, for example, "What will it cost me?" They fail to get a handle on the upside of sacrifice. Sacrifice establishes commitment to one's direction; sacrifice reinforces purpose in one's direction; sacrifice instills pride in one's direction.

You will notice that directionless people seldom exhibit personal pride. The reality is that they have little self-esteem because their lives lack a defined sense of purpose. Investment in your dream is a tangible representation of your commitment to your dream, and thus, aligns you more strongly with a purpose in life.

To the short-sighted, sacrifice is to be lamented. For the dream-sighted, sacrifice is honor. It's the sign that you've gone beyond just talking. It's the sign that you're on the road—the road which leads you to the prize of which you have already placed a deposit. Take pride in that.

Attending inspirational conferences and rallies dramatically increase a person's resolve in fighting the dragons that block the pathway to success. Yet, I hear people give legitimate reasons for why they can't afford to attend these inspirational functions even though the exercise is intended to build a foundation for further business. I must admit to having used these same words myself, ". . . I can't afford to. . . I can't afford to. . . I can't afford to. . . " One day, I realized that the banner over my world read: "I can't afford to..." It sickened me because the more I said it, the more it was becoming a self-fulfilling prophecy. The way to leave the world of "I can't afford to" is to utter the words "I can't afford *not to*".

Let a friend of mine share his story of overcoming this struggle:

Dear Wes,

I remember you speaking recently about investing in your dream as a sign of commitment to your dream. About six months ago I had the chance to test out your theory. I was invited to go to a trade conference that was billed as an event that would help me to achieve my goals in business. The big difficulty was that the one-day conference had a price tag equivalent to the cost of feeding my family for six weeks. Added to this was the fact that the conference was being held in a city four hours drive from my home, not to mention losing a day's income in attending the conference. Having just started out in business, writing the check for the conference registration took me three days. It was a big struggle to commit the funds by signing the check and posting it.

Well, the day of the conference arrived. I seated myself in the auditorium and took notes about what the speakers were saying, all the time hoping they would say something that would justify my investment. Yet, it was over the morning coffee break that I struck gold. Being invited with all the other delegates to look over the trade fair at the back of the auditorium, I met a company representative that manufactured products like I used extensively in my business. I had never heard of his company but when he asked for the opportunity to submit a quote for my next order, I thought there was nothing to lose. Since I was needing to re-order soon, I told him to get on it right away. He did and a day later submitted his quote.

A few weeks later the product was supplied in as good a quality as my previous supplier, but for much less. In fact the money I saved is equivalent to feeding my family for nineteen weeks. So the way I figure it, investing in that one day conference meant that for thirteen weeks my family eats for free!

Thanks for encouraging me to see that investing in your dream pays.

The explicit benefit of opening your wallet to an inspirational environment is not only in the inspiration that you receive, it also becomes a badge that you can wear with pride. A badge which says, "I believe in my dream. . . and I'm willing to put my money where my mouth is." Implicitly, you are proving to yourself that the connection you have with your dream is not just talk, but a real action-based personal investment. Ultimately, that is what a good relationship requires.

◆

Stage 5

Deciding to Go For It

(Engaging the Dream)

◆

> The strength of your commitment is decided by the good things you pass over for the sake of that which you really want.

DECIDING TO GO for it? You can be excused for asking: "Haven't we already done this by investing in the dream? Surely, getting to the point of sinking your resources into a dream is ample indication of going for it?!" The answer to this really requires an examination of what the term 'going for it' actually means. Yes, to invest in a dream is an indication of your commitment. To a certain extent you are going for it, but, there is another threshold of commitment that awaits your crossing. Until you have crossed this threshold, you can't really say that you've become engaged to your dream.

You are going for it when you reach that point where you say to yourself, "This one's the one. . . it's the one I choose *above* the others!" You cross this line when you make the decision to quit scratching away at the goal, and instead, tear into it with absolute conviction. Up to this point you have really just nibbled, albeit you've found it nourishing enough, but, when you become engaged, it's like taking the bite of your life. Some people describe this as 'hitting the hot button.' Whatever you choose to call it, one thing is for certain—you can't call it an option. Anyone serious about reaching their dream goal has to cross this line of engagement-like commitment.

Desire Management

If you sat down and wrote a list of all the things you desire in life, you'll quickly discover the abundance of desires competing for your time.

Initially, there is nothing unusual or wrong with this. When it comes to our desires, we usually have many pots on the stove at once which all could be considered legitimate interests. To a certain extent, this is what creates the interest factor in life. Having many fires going at once keeps us from being bored by monotony. It can be quite exciting keeping all the fires burning.

However, that which makes life interesting can easily make life seem out of control when you realize that your life is ablaze with desires, each calling upon your time and asking for your attention.

Attending to making all your dreams come true is like a circus performer endeavoring to keep all the plates in the air and spinning. What starts as the exciting situation of having many things upon which you can choose to concentrate, escalates to the point where relating to your desires becomes overwhelming. Your life begins to resemble the work of an air-traffic controller at Chicago's O'Hare Airport, with so many planes in the air and knowing that it is up to you to guide each one into a successful landing.

What stops people from successfully guiding their dream into the land of reality is they have too many dreams in the air at once.

Any person of greatness is well aware of the burden of choice. They choose to neglect some things for the benefit of something else. And therein lies the principle: The person who wants something intensely enough realizes that there comes a time when they have to apply more energy to that one desire than what they've been giving. And to give it more energy, they know they're going to have to get the fuel from somewhere.

Such is my enthusiasm for achievement, I sometimes catch myself wishing that someone would re-define how many hours make a day. Instead of twenty-four hours a day, perhaps they could make it thirty-two hours. This would give me the chance to get more fires started and give me more time to keep them going.

Knowing that increasing the hours in a day would require the changing of the unchangeable laws of the universe, I then turn to wishing someone would give me their left over energy that they haven't used in the day. This, too, is implausible. How many people do you know who think they have energy to spare? Even inactive people and non-achievers still manage to fill their time with what they feel is important activity.

The reality for most of us is that in order to apply more energy to a goal, we have to obtain it by redirecting it from elsewhere within our lives. In other words we decide to shut down our energy in some areas and re-route that energy to the desire for which we have hit the hot button.

In building a good relationship with your desire, the experience requires you to learn how to analyze personal fuel consumption. Do not confuse this with time management. It is possible to have your time managed perfectly across the face of many activities and aspirations and still travel no closer to your dream. Taking command of your personal fuel budget is all about desire management. In order to make possible the things that you really want in life, you have to shut the fuel flow valve to the desires that are on the fringe of your life. Re-route as much energy as possible to those dreams 'in the zone' of your life. This will mean saying goodbye to some interests.

Forsaking All Others

I make a point of associating with people of positive orientation. However, there are times when I am puzzled why some of them do not have more specific achievements on the board. Their orientation leads me to believe they are capable of great things, yet their score board looks meager. I could assume their lack of performance is due to a lack of effort. This assumption though, is proved lacking when I am reminded of others who do not work as hard but score much more. Then, perhaps their lack of performance is due to a lower educational standing. The same invariably happens. Someone is discovered with much less education but with more results.

When we try to account for performance due to natural ability, luck, the position or state of the market, we are always proved wrong. There is always someone with less who ends up achieving more! They achieve more because they forsake more. Part of the work is saying goodbye to those attractions which are not in the zone. Study their lives and you'll see that they've honed their desires until they fit in the zone, then they direct as much energy as they can to that zone. Forsaking fringe desires means they can focus on the desires located in their zone.

Recently, I was watching a television broadcast of an international athletics contest. The world champion English sprinter, Lindford Christie, was running in the one-hundred meter sprint race. At the end of the track, the sponsoring television network had placed a camera to enable viewers to watch the facial expressions of the sprinters as they made their way toward the finishing line. It was interesting to watch the face of Lindford Christie. His eyes were opened wider than the eyes of all the other runners. He was mesmerized in his view of the finish line. True, he must have been experiencing all the challenges of physical exertion as with all the other runners. Yet while the faces of the others exhibited the stress of exertion, Christie's face hailed nothing but a controlled fixation with the end goal. He won.

The ability of a person to achieve great things is based on their ability to fix their eyes on their goal and not be diverted—even by *good* things. One of the most sensible pieces of advice that any motivator gives is this: *sometimes you have to say no to the good, in order to say yes to the best.* This is strange advice when you consider that when we are growing up, we are taught that the key to a right life is to avoid the bad. Now we're advocating the key to success is avoiding the good!

When it comes down to it, avoiding the bad does not lead to success. It merely ensures survival. You want to do more than this. Making life grand assumes that one avoids the bad, and gets on with prioritizing the good. Prioritizing the good means making the tough decisions as to which good things are going to be set aside to create a clear view of that one thing you want more than anything. So many great dreams are snatched from becoming reality, not by bad things getting in the way, but by the good things getting in the way.

Choosing between good and bad is easy because it really involves choosing according to the mandates of your conscience. In choosing between good things, you do not have the benefit of your conscience helping in the decision, because according to your conscience, all options are morally right.

An understanding and commitment to the zone principle throws deciding light onto the right choice between good options. Many good aspirations will be terminated because they're not *in the zone*. Those who make such courageous decisions discover the power in being good stewards of their energy. As a result, they end up with significant 'touch-downs' on the scoreboard of life.

Neglecting a few good options for the sake of your ultimate goal is a reliable way of measuring your intensity for the desired goal. If deciding to 'go for it' does not require the sacrifice of at least a few other worthy goals, then it's a good indication that you have set your sights on something so deficient of challenge that its dream status is questionable.

To be in an engaged state means that you have forsaken other worthy activities and goals. For the sake of concentrating your resources, you have decided to bid them farewell, knowing that by doing so, you can give more energy and focus to your desires in the zone.

Giving It Full Power But Not All Power

What's the difference, I hear you ask? Let me use this illustration to help explain. For years I have enjoyed the friendship of an air force jet fighter pilot. In talking to him about his work as a squadron leader, I have come to learn a few things about the way an FA-18 jet airplane operates.

With regard to power capacity, a jet airplane

can be operating at full power but still have extra power in reserve in the form of 'afterburners'. Occasionally, jet airplanes can be in a situation where they are operating at full power but need extra power to get them out of a tight situation. At this point, the pilot can dump a load of fuel straight into the exhaust. Since the exhaust is already running hot, the injected fuel ignites, creating a massive boost to the plane's thrust. However there is a downside to this mode of operation. Though creating scintillating performance, utilizing the afterburners expends massive amounts of fuel. So much so, that prolonged use will quickly exhaust the airplane's fuel supply.

It is possible that we can operate in the same way. We can throw our lives into over-drive using our adrenaline afterburners. While this is necessary on some occasions, it is incredibly hazardous to develop a lifestyle of becoming dependent on these reserves for normal operation. Give it full power, yes, but if you want to last the distance, be wary of the dangers in giving it all your power.

At full power consider yourself in a state of maximum concentration. Anything beyond that and you're heading into the territory of having your dream dominate you instead of developing you. Being dominated by something leaves you too open to humiliating yourself because somewhere along the line, you've lost focus of who you are.

Soon after we were married, Eleanor and I found ourselves in the situation of needing a second car. After doing the rounds of the local car dealers, I had narrowed the selection down to a few options. It was time to take a test drive. The salesman accompanied me and continued to give me his best sales pitch as I drove out of the car lot.

He knew I was interested in the car, and he was working overtime to convince me that I should buy it. Getting back to the yard, I expressed a few reservations about the car. The salesman started to get agitated, as if he had exhausted his list of sales pitches. Finally, in desperation, he blurted out, "C'mon man, I haven't had a sale all week and I really need a sale to keep on the right side with my boss." He knew the moment he said it, that he'd lost his grip on the situation and also lost the sale.

The desire to make a sale had so dominated him that it caused him to make himself vulnerable to humiliation. Walking away, I knew the value of his life was greater than whether he made a sale or not. However, in the heat of the moment, so consumed by the goal of making a sale, he had lost touch on that reality. The badge of *going for it* is not humiliation.

An Engagement Ring

I am a great believer in having external representations that symbolize an inward commitment. The classic example of this is the engagement ring. To an engaged couple, the value of a diamond ring is far in excess of its value as a piece of jewelry. It is what this piece of jewelry *represents* that holds the greatest value. Namely, that a decision has been made by two people in love to commit to an important course of action—the joining of their lives in matrimony. The engagement ring thus stands as a sign to all that someone has decided to go for it! A symbol of commitment.

I drive a car that is really no more than a weary set of wheels dragging its tired old body around town in its last years of service to the age of transportation. Any pride it was able to afford its owner was relinquished amidst the onset of rust and frequent mechanical breakdown, not to mention its body style giving away its age to the embarrassing 1970's era of fashion. In short, it's a heap! But to me, it is my symbol of engagement. It is my symbol of commitment to a dream which I have set myself toward achieving.

It's not that I could not afford a new car. In fact, I could buy a fleet of new cars. Why do I

96

choose to stick with my old car? Simply because right now I want a physical reminder of commitment to my dream more than I want a new car.

Every time I get into this car and fire up its tired old engine, it reminds me that I am committed to my dream regardless of how tired I feel. As I drive it down the road being tossed around in response to every bump, it serves to remind me that the road toward any worthwhile dream is inevitably bumpy. On cold days when I wished its heater worked, I imagine how warm I will feel in my heart when my dream comes true. When it breaks down, it reminds me to be not surprised that sometimes there are interruptions to the schedule of a dream coming true. When I feel embarrassed driving such a vagrant vehicle, I remind myself that true greatness is not in the car that you drive, but in what you are willing to forego to make your dream come true.

Admittedly, there are days when I feel like going out and buying a flashy car, telling myself I can afford it and what's more, I deserve it. But in doing so, it would mean sacrificing my badge of commitment to my greater dream. On one occasion, I offered a friend a ride. As he positioned himself in the passenger seat, he made a comment about it making good financial sense to drive the cheapest car one's pride would allow!

Yes, I drive this heap of a car with pride but not for what it is, but for what it represents—my symbol of commitment to a great dream. One day this great dream will come true. When it does, that commitment symbolizing car will find its rest, and you'll find me in the driver's seat of a party on wheels! Wooaaah. . .

In building a good relationship with your desire, you need to have a physical symbol which helps you positively relate to your desire. A symbol which reminds you that you are serious about your commitment to the dream. A symbol which will remind you why you want your dream to come true. Something that will remind you that you are engaged and going for it.

Engagement symbols not only benefit you by reminding you of the harvest for which you are headed, they also empower you. I know people who could afford to update, upgrade, take the cash, or receive the dividends now. But though they could, they choose not to. They know that to delay the gratification of taking the reward now will result in a better reward down the track. An engagement symbol symbolizes the fact that you are in the the position of power. It is a reminder that you have exercised your power to delay 'payday'—knowing that there is better outcome in store for having exercised your power.

In viewing your engagement symbol as a physical representation of your restraint from 'cashing in,' you are empowered. Restraint is an exhibition of strength. To delay the payday will make the future more significant for you and the ones you love. Your engagement symbol is a physical reminder of your commitment to this principle.

In a profound way, your engagement symbol is a motivation for keeping your focus on track with your goal. Instead of harvesting at the first sign of fruit, your symbol of engagement empowers you with the knowledge that as long as you keep on track, harvest is inevitable. You can't miss out. The engagement symbol reminds you that the big day is on its way. Not only that, but when it does arrive, it will be bursting to be harvested.

Stage 6

Winning the Fight with Frustration

(Waiting For the Big Day)

◆

> Success is reserved for those who develop the art of staying on course when the journey is taking longer than anticipated.

RECENTLY I WAS IN ANOTHER city on a speaking assignment. Attending the week-long conference meant being three thousand miles away from Eleanor and the boys. I took comfort in knowing that the conclusion of the conference on Friday night would present me with my plane ride back home to see them. Things had gone so well during the week, that on the day before my scheduled departure, the head of the organization asked me to postpone my return home with the invitation to give another keynote address over the weekend. It was a prestigious event and naturally, I was flattered to be asked— not to mention the financial incentive offered was considerably enticing.

This being the case however, the overriding feeling about the invitation unsettled me. Why? Because all week I had my sights set on Friday night being the finish line. The offer to stay back and give the keynote address felt like someone was postponing the event I was anticipating, that of being reunited with home. It's a little disconcerting when you've been running a marathon to find that just as you're heading around the last bend, someone relocates the finish line.

The time prior to your dream coming true can often deal you this type of experience, not only once, but repeatedly. You are ready for your dream to materialize, you are ready to victoriously throw yourself across the finish line, but you look up to discover it's going to take longer than the time frame you had first set your hopes on. A voice inside you tells you to be patient, but it's not commanding enough to dispel a 'hit squad' of demoralizing thoughts and discouraging feelings.

In the stages we go through in our relationship with our dream, this one seems to take the most time and therefore, is the hardest. This stage issues us with the challenge of patience. You don't need to be told that surviving this stage is crucial. You know this. The person who doesn't give up is the one who eventually lands the prize. What we need to know, more than anything, is how to survive this frustrating time.

When you have set your sights on a dream, it's only natural that you wonder when the dream will come true. Our hope is that it will be sooner rather than later. The reality is that it often comes later rather than sooner. So how do we keep our dream alive when it seems as far off as ever? How do we keep the fire fueled when the 'low fuel light' of our enthusiasm starts to flash? How do we keep our spirit up in the face of the challenges and failures that we face on the way? Within the answers to these questions lies further power to help us last the distance toward our dreams becoming reality. As you read, weave these empowering thoughts into the fabric of your relationship with your dream.

Keeping The Fire Burning When It's Raining

The all-time great basketball player, Michael Jordan, talks of the fuel that can be extracted out of failure. This is a somewhat strange phenomenon, but nonetheless, it is true. Sometimes following a failure, we can feel a new surge of energy. The type of energy that makes you say "Okay, you won round one. . . but I'm NOT DEFEATED, I'm coming back. . . somebody ring the bell for round two!"

It would be great if one experienced this positive effect every time there was a setback. Unfortunately, you don't, and particularly when you feel you've been going at it for a long time. The more exasperated you feel, the more likely setbacks will de-motivate you. Sometimes you're able to take the fuel out of challenges to help propel you forward. Others times, the fuel merely floods your engine to a grinding halt. What makes the difference?

There can be many factors, but generally, we are more resilient in the first few rounds of the match than we are the later ones. Enthusiasm helps us get back up the first few times. After that, it takes something more. This is where the strength of our relationship with our dream comes to the rescue.

The work we have done in developing that relationship now starts to help us. We know why we chose our dream. We have calculated its mutual benefits to all areas of our life. We like who we become through our commitment to the dream. The relationship thus keeps the dream alive. It keeps the fire burning. It keeps us on course.

Building On Your Foundation

During this important stage, when enthusiasm is no longer adequate in strength to get us through, the relationship will. This is our solid foundation. It's upon this foundation that two key components for survival are built. Namely, **positive mental anchors** and **positive activities**. Analyzing how people remain buoyant during the time it takes for their dreams to come true, has led me to discover that they fully utilize these two survival components.

Having built a solid foundation in forming a good relationship with your dream, going on to incorporate these two survival components will enable you to relate more positively to the challenges, instead of being demoralized by them.

COMPONENT ONE
Positive Mental Anchors

When the fulfillment of your desire is delayed, it does, at times, affect your feelings of self-worth. Just as it's natural that your confidence inflates when things go well, conversely, when reality falls short of expectation, air escapes from the balloon of your confidence.

When feeling deflated, you begin to ask probing questions about your ability or the validity of your motivation, and whether you've been 'realistic' in your assessment of the probability of your dream materializing. These self-probing exercises may seem innocent and rational enough, but at this stage you're more prone to come to negative conclusions than positive ones. Usually, in the face of discouragement, one's mind settles upon the least positive thoughts that one's self esteem will allow.

It's times like these that, more than ever, you need to harness your thinking process and connect it to positive mental anchors. These anchors are principles that time and experience has proven to be true. They become steadfast anchors that you can latch your mind onto when the circumstances start to push you around. Next to knowing these principles, is the need to pre-set them in your mind, ready to be employed when needed. When the going gets tough, encouraging thoughts need to be conveniently found. When you are down, you don't have the energy to go searching for elusive truths.

Especially when you are being pelted by the storms of discouraging feelings, a storehouse of positive mental thoughts is just what's required to protect you from the attack of disparaging feelings that challenge you about whether it's worth going on. We can not avoid times of mental stormy weather, but we can insure ourselves against its affect by having some anchors to stop us from going adrift. Here are seven anchors that will help you to stay on course and keep the fire of your dream burning.

1. A diamond is what becomes of ordinary coal that endures time and pressure.

When it comes to determining the time when our dream will come true, we are confronted with part of a dream's nature— the intangibility of its arrival time. We know that for those who do not quit, a dream will eventually materialize. That's not the problem. It's not knowing the *when* that almost kills us! People want to know when closure will take place. When a date is not forthcoming, it adds intangibility to an important part of our lives. It is aggravating and can even make a person sick.

One of the things I love to do around the house is to work with concrete. While Eleanor is content with pruning and pulling weeds, she jests that my intolerance for such gardening is attributed to a secret fetish I have for concrete. One day, while mixing up another batch of sand and cement, I pondered why it was that I preferred pouring concrete to other work around the house. After a little self analysis, I realized that it was because so much of my life was dealing with intangibles. Though my professional activities are immensely gratifying, the activities do lack the tangible qualities of concrete.

For instance, not every song I write is worth performing. Not every artistic project that I embark upon turns out according to my plan. Not every one of my investments gives me a thrilling return. Not every contact in business produces business. Not every person that I reach out to help becomes the person I know they're capable of becoming. But, you can be darn sure that every batch of concrete I mix hardens and stays there forever! It's that quality that I like. It's that quality that I wish extended to the work of attaining our noble desires.

If only the journey towards our dreams coming true was like working with concrete. We could simply add water to the right ingredients, mix, pour, set, leave. . . and within twenty-four hours, it's there for life! No, the laws of life and personal development come packaged with some uncertainty and untimely interruptions during the journey. The rewards of succeeding become the specially reserved prize for those who prove their toughness in the face of these interruptions by enduring.

All who aspire to do great things go through times of having to patiently 'hang in there.' But keep in mind that time and pressure transforms you in the process. Diamonds are formed ninety miles inside the earth, the pressure of which is equal to the weight of twenty elephants! You can easily identify people who are diamonds in the making. They are the ones that cheerfully proceed knowing that by enduring the tough times and pressure they are in the process of becoming diamonds.

2. Prospering those whom I esteem is the grand result of my worthy dream.

When challenged with frustrating delays, ask yourself if frustration is sufficient a reason to terminate your course of action, and with it, the good that people would experience because you endured the delay? If your dream can result in blessing other people's lives, then isn't it something worth protecting from being snatched away by something that is most times temporary?

Some time ago, I returned from a nine-week national tour planning to settle in at home for a few weeks rest. Eleanor and I had discussed what I could do during this time. We decided it was time to enclose our backyard with a fence. It had been a goal of ours for years, but the growing interest of our little boy for the great outdoors led to the realization that the project was quite overdue.

Had our house been built on land that was flat, I could have immediately commenced erecting the fence. But since we were situated on the side of a hill, I first had to build a retaining wall so that the yard resembled something a little more user-friendly than a ski slope. I had watched enough episodes of 'Home Improvement' to be positively dangerous.

Armed with a shovel and a tape measure, I headed into the back yard. Basically all I had to do was dig eleven holes, about four feet deep, all in a straight line. Simple. . .

The first hole took longer than I thought, so to celebrate its completion, I paused for refreshments. The second hole took me through to lunch. Rejuvenated by lunch, I attacked the third hole with passionate vengeance only to discover a tree root half a shovel below the surface. Trying to dig around it, I quickly discovered that this was no tree root. . . maybe it was the tree itself. The more I tried to budge this obstacle, the more I realized that this was no tree. It could very well have been Noah's Ark come to rest in the depths of my back yard!

Having ruined most every power tool that I owned trying to dislodge the stubborn obstacle, I sat down beside the hole feeling defeated. Just then Eleanor emerged from the house to enthusiastically ask, "How are you doing, honey?" The truth was I wasn't 'doing' at all. I was frustrated and feeling burned out like my poor circular saw which had just given up its life in dedicated servitude to my dogged determination.

Eleanor quickly retreated into the house sensing that she needed to work on her timing. I sat there and wondered whether it would be easier to sell the house and buy another one—this time with a finished back yard included.

As I approached the third hole (by now the back yard was looking like a demolition site) I thought to myself, "Had I known that I was going to run into this much difficulty, I would never have started in the first place." Does this sound familiar?

The truth is that in every journey there is the inevitability of some unexpected obstacles and delays. As much as we all prefer to avoid them, sometimes we just can't. When this happens, alter your approach if you must, but ultimately **keep digging!** The happiest people are not the ones who pursue a life avoiding challenges, but the ones who endure the challenges and turn them into conquests.

Though it took much longer to build than I first anticipated, when I look out on a backyard of laughing children, I am reminded that any goal that can bring blessing to others is a goal worth the perseverance. The best desires are the ones that make for a better life for those dearest to you. So, the next time you're tempted to give up in the heat of difficulty, remind yourself that by strengthening your grip, you are building a legacy of prosperity and honor for those you love.

Someone once told me, "Don't let the darkness of the valley steal the vision of what you clearly saw on the mountain." Next time you catch yourself thinking, "Had I known it was going to be this tough I never would have started," think about what you saw on the mountain when you began your pilgrimage. Think of those who will benefit if you don't give up while in the shadows of the valley.

3. Frustration is a flare that you're going somewhere.

The pathway of least resistance is the road that the majority of people travel. When you see the crowd going in your direction, you know this is the signal that you are on such a road. The pathway to dream-inspired greatness, however, is the road less travelled because it is harder. The signal that you are on this pathway is the difficulty and frustrations that you experience along the way.

Having a dream will inevitably cause you to go through personal trials that will test your patience and resolve. I wish it were not so. If only it were the case that when we signed up to go for a dream, we were given a solid contract which listed the exact date that the dream would become reality. Given that this is not the case, we are left with a journey where our travelling companion is frustration. Anyone who has contemplated these words "It's taking longer than I first thought," is well acquainted with the company of such a companion.

The first reaction when we are feeling frustrated at the lack of progress is to think to ourselves "something is wrong!" Well, in all honesty, there could be something that needs to be modified in order to proceed toward your goal, but feelings of frustration are not necessarily the sign that something is wrong. On the contrary, times of frustration are perfectly normal.

Delays and detours are part of the territory of the journey toward a destination rich in reward. Show me a person who does not experience frustration and I'll show you a person who is going nowhere.

The person who has a good relationship with a dream sees delays and detours not as enemies, but as essential indicators that they're on the right track. They doggedly 'hang in there' because they know that a smooth and uninterrupted journey is really no journey at all. The goal of such a journey is not worth it, because it does not expand you in the process. If the goal doesn't stretch you, then it's not taking you anywhere significant. The value of a destination is determined by the challenges faced to get there. Feelings of frustration only attend those who are pushing the limits, going places they have never been before. Remind yourself that frustration is a flare signaling that you're not leading a static, boring life, but rather a life of discovering opportunities to energize you into greatness.

4. The bigger the test the better the testimony.

Good ambassadors of success know that while the symbols of their success can be impressive, it's not the symbols which inspire. Assets create an impression, but the story of how personal mountains were conquered in achieving victory is what really inspires people. It is the account of what struggles were contended with on the journey to victory which gives people's hearts a lift.

Hearing successful people talk about their lean times; hearing them share about the times when their 'belief' was battered; hearing them give account of the detours and delays; to be told of the days they felt like giving up in the face of obstacles, but didn't; it's hearing these things which inspires others to survive their hard times.

True, the attractive assets of the successful person are impressive, but it's hearing about the inferno they went through on their journey that holds the true inspirational value for others trying to do the same.

You can't lead people through territory over which you've never been. Imagine if you got everything you wanted exactly when you wanted. How irrelevant your life would be to others. Real people go through real struggles, and if you have never struggled, real people will not be able to relate to your life in an inspirational way. The more you are tested, the more inspiring your testimony will be to others.

5. Giving up may bring relief, but it never brings reward.

Yes, there are some things I have given up on. When the going got tough—I quit! Upon doing so, I felt a sense of relief, but never in an inspirational way. Giving up would never motivate me to phone my friends and say, "Hey! Guess what? I just quit trying something that I hoped I could do!"

While initially quitting may bring relief, this quickly gives way to feeling remorse because you've lost something—for in giving away the dream, you give away the sense of destiny and direction that your dream put in place. The by-product of a dream is seen in one's drive, determination and sense of purpose. Quitting may bring temporary relief from the pain of endeavor, but in doing so, it introduces a void into one's life. We can't assume that taking away the pain automatically ushers in joy. In reality, it ushers in emptiness. Unless a new dream ignites one's energy, coping with a void has a pain all of its own.

I enjoy travelling the world speaking words of encouragement and hope into people's lives. Telling stories of my own personal experience is my greatest resource in being able to inspire people. But I have never been able to inspire anyone with a story that ends with my decision to quit. There is no inspirational value in it, because quitting is the most natural thing to do. It's something that we don't need to be taught, nor motivated to do.

The most succulent taste of life is the reward of having fought, endured, and conquered. People never get tired of relating to that. Temporary relief from pain is a poor substitute for the reward in achieving your goals.

6. If you keep with the quest, you'll become friends with the best.

Our ability to keep our spirit buoyant is increased when we are reminded that we are not alone in our quest. Solitude has its place, but within the scope of this stage, solitude is not a good state to be in for extended periods of time. When we connect with people who are going through or who have gone through our current experience, energizing support is found in the connection. You realize that you are not alone. Indeed you are part of an elite club of mountain conquerors on the move.

Experiencing setback while in solitude leaves you vulnerable to the antagonism of your disappointment. Remind yourself that your predicament gives you much in common with other go-getters. Suffering the challenges of this stage gives you the privilege of being able to rub shoulders with the elite, knowing that your experience qualifies you as one of them.

7. If the process has pain, the success won't be vain.

There is a need for maturity to handle success when it comes. Delays and detours serve to mature you. There is nothing as frail as immature success. Surviving the challenges gives your experience thoughtful perspective and helps you to position pride in the right place in your life. Without this, you become too vulnerable to the havoc that unbridled pride can cause.

It is possible that when goals are achieved to respond to the excitement in a counter-productive way. Prideful, arrogant success is a posture that leads to a fall. The net result is that you become a poor ambassador for success.

Trials and struggle along the trek have a way of diffusing our natural inclination of becoming arrogant and conceited. We have all come across prima donnas inflated with self-importance. Pain along the way helps us to realize we are not invincible, and saves us from such a debilitating complex.

The world-class performer Garth Brooks is the most personable artist I have ever seen interviewed. In talking about his life, he recounted recently how he was glad that he did not have the chiselled features of a Greek god. He said that the challenges of hair loss and weight control have helped him handle his massive success more maturely. Though his immense status gives him the right to parade an aura of invincibility, he doesn't. He views it all as a blessing. That's why Garth Brooks is an inspiration to me and millions of others. His journey was rough at times, but you can tell it has had a positive effect on how well he relates to people. The humility of the winner is born in the waiting.

These are some of the many positive mental anchors that can stop us from coming adrift amidst the mental storms that will inevitably beset us prior to our dreams materializing. More often than not, in retrospect, we are able to clearly see benefits that grew out of the delays and setbacks. Until knowledge of those benefits come to light, our task should be to just keep putting one foot after the other, always in line with our plan. So, in reality, we are never 'waiting' for our dreams to come true; rather, we are progressing until our dreams come true.

COMPONENT TWO

Positive Activities

Remaining buoyant during the time it takes for your dream to come true requires you to remain active. Nothing feeds the potential for your dreams to bewilder you more than periods of inactivity.

Sometimes, even a well planned schedule can break down, leading to periods where you have frustrating time on your hands. You must keep active. It is vital that you have a list of specific positive activities ready to employ. Doing these activities will give you strong encouragement that you are still moving forward and being fruitful with your time.

Anticipate temporary lapses in progress to achieving your dream. Don't be left scratching your head in idleness. This only exacerbates feelings of frustration. Where idleness has the uncanny ability to steer you into the valley of frustration, activity steers you out of such a valley. Put together your own list of activities. You may include some of the following activities which have helped me immensely.

1. Formulate a P.I.E. list.
(People I Encourage list)

The quickest antidote for dealing with negative feelings about your situation is to move your focus off yourself and on to another person. Consider the fact that if you have trying times, many others must go through similar times. Probably millions.

Become an expert at encouraging people. To be most effective, choose a manageable list (my list contains ten people), and make them the special targets of your encouragement. Set yourself up as the special envoy of encouragement to this small band of people. Custom tailor a way to lift their spirits, their visions, their dreams. You will be uplifted having done so. Don't forget to include a few people of distinguished success status. Successful people still appreciate positive regard and encouragement.

2. Contact your P.I.E. list.

Receiving an encouraging fax, letter, or card, has the potential to turn someone's day around. It doesn't need to be a manifesto on positive mental attitude. In fact, a few sentences from the heart is much more effective. Simply express why you appreciate them and why you admire what they are doing.

It is sad that in this age of communication superhighways, we are actually communicating fewer personal messages than ever. Think about what comes into your mail box each day. The percentage of mail that connects us personally with the heart of another person is hardly quantifiable. Yes, we have never communicated so much information and at a speed previously inconceivable. Yet, we have never been so hungry to hear from each other personal messages. I am convinced we need to send more personal communiques to each other, with no other agenda than to let someone know we care about them.

If you are compelled to start this practice, here is a tip. Write by hand. This conveys much more warmth, regardless of neatness!

Having deposited some kindness into the lives of those on your P.I.E. list, may not, at the end of the day, have positioned you any closer to your dream. But there is every possibility that you have helped someone move another step closer to theirs.

3. Walk.

Today everyone acknowledges the need for physical exercise. Some people lament that eight hours of sleep stands between them and their 5 AM five-mile run. I wish I could share their lament. My record for early morning runs is not that impressive.

Generally speaking, in the first tri-mester of one's life, exercise is not a serious issue. While some are blessed with high metabolism all their life, for most of us there comes a time when we're sent definite warning signals. Signals that inform us that our slowing metabolism is sending us in the direction toward a larger clothes size.

Wanting to avoid this, over the years I have engaged in several forms of aerobic exercise; jogging, swimming, tennis, squash, low and high impact aerobics, to name a few, none with which I was able to form a lasting affinity. The one form of exercise that has stuck with me is the one that I enjoy the most—WALKING. Old fashioned, maybe, but according to fitness experts, highly effective. Often I load one of my boys into the stroller and take him for a fun ride in the process.

In conjunction with a low fat, low sugar intake, walking has a desirable effect physically. It also has incredible impact mentally. Not only does it increase fitness, walking does something to stimulate fresh thinking. Some of my most creative ideas come when I venture out that front door and swagger in the direction of fitness. You may not derive solutions out of every walk, but this positive activity is more likely to refresh your mind, than staying in the environment where anxiety first besets you.

4. Keep a Journal.

Writing the words expressing what you are going through is therapeutic, but its value doesn't stop there. As you experience victories, you place yourself in a position where you will be called upon to talk about your successes. If you have written down your experiences during your journey, this becomes a valuable tool in preparing what you will say when called upon. Journals are a good way to re-connect with some thoughts that you have long since forgotten in the wake of your success. Every day for the past fifteen years, I have continued the practice of journalling my experience. Except for five days that for various reasons I missed recording my thoughts of the day, I have an irreplaceable record of experiences that help me in relating to others.

5. Read.

Of this I do not need to convince you, for you are currently engaged in doing just that. However, when you're feeling exasperated about the time it's taking for your dream to materialize, it's often hard to get motivated to read a motivational book. Have you ever been slumped in a mental malaise, knowing that reading something positive would help you, but you just cannot muster the energy to pick up a book and start reading? This can even further your 'down' condition. What can you do to escape this mental malaise?

First, don't be alarmed as this happens to even the most motivated people. Sometimes, we wake to find ourselves in a lethargic state, and what's more, we're not even sure how we got there! Friends of mine call this condition 'flatlining.' Do not think that you are less of a person because you have occasionally found yourself in this condition. The condition is not critical if you submit yourself to this exercise—READING!

One of the main causes of mental malaise is mental staleness—our thoughts are stagnant and lack the capacity to carry our mind in a fresh direction. There is nothing like reading the ideas of others to rectify this.

Learning from people whose lives are a testimony to having survived, though the odds were against them, re-fuels our spirit. Reading books that convey their ideas and tell of their pilgrimage helps us to tap into revitalizing power so we can, once again, forge ahead.

6. Design how you'll celebrate your success.

When the Boeing aircraft company launched the newly designed 777 aircraft, they threw a party for the ten-thousand employees responsible for the effort. The light show and video presentation of the unveiling was breath-taking. Without doubt, it took months to organize. It was evident that even before the aircraft's completion, part of the Boeing team were concentrating on organizing the celebration.

There is nothing to stop us from doing the same. Long before reaching a goal, I am often planning how I am going to celebrate the occasion. It's a positive activity that can keep you buoyant in a lull.

7. Visit a champion.

Visiting someone you admire is an activity that will breathe fresh air into your dream. The only difficulty, however, is getting the appointment! Champions value time and their privacy. The last thing they desire is to be harassed by people wanting to 'sun-bake' in their aura. However, this does not mean it is impossible. In fact, a few steps can open the door to their heart and create a positive impression, even a lasting friendship.

Step One: Write a well prepared letter introducing yourself. Write no more than one page, but enough to convey confidence that you're not a starry-eyed member of the paparazzi who wants to consume their valuable time.

Step Two: Politely ask to see them for twenty minutes maximum. If this time is extended, it must only be at the champion's initiative. (I once drove eighteen hours to spend twenty minutes with someone whose counsel I aspired to gain. It was a trip that I still benefit from today.)

Step Three: Prepare three questions that you feel only this person could address. Don't blow the time asking questions your mother could answer!

Step Four: Make the meeting as stress-free as possible for them. Let them choose the time and place. An invitation to take them to a restaurant of their choice can be a compelling offer, as well as buying you extra time.

Step Five: Take a gift as an expression of your gratitude for their time. It can be something for them, their partner, or children. The gift doubles as a thank you and as a tangible reminder of your meeting, long after you're gone. Be careful not to go overboard in lavishness, as this will have the reverse effect—making the recipient feel uncomfortable. Remember the ancient proverb: *A gift opens the way for the giver and ushers him into the presence of the great. (Prov.18:16)*

8. Visit a symbol of your dream.

One of my dreams has been to give my family the experience of living in another country. You can imagine the organization required to facilitate the realization of such a dream. Often prolonged times of waiting, while embassies and foreign bureaucratic departments processed applications, made us feel that our plans were getting nowhere.

On one occasion when I was personally questioning whether the dream would ever come true, I loaded the family into the car and headed to the international airport. We spent the day watching jumbo jets land and take off. Somehow, the smell of aviation fuel and the sight of hundreds of people heading off to exotic places refreshed the desire to keep on track with our plans.

Is there some place you can go, or some person you can see that would somehow symbolize your dream? Don't sit at home wallowing in inactivity. Get up! Go visit a symbol! Stay actively involved in your dream.

9. Do something romantic.

When it comes to traffic delays, I much prefer detours to jams. At least with detours you feel like you're still on the move. I feel the same way with 'dream delays'. Detours are better than jams.

If you feel like the progress towards your dream has stalled, then take advantage of the delay and take a 'love detour'. Use the time to pour some romantic fuel onto the fire of your love life. At the end of the day, you may be no closer to your dream, but you will be closer to the one you love!

When was the last time you planned an act of romance for someone special? This question is especially aimed at those with young children. Those of you in this stage of life know that your little toddlers were born with an in-built capacity to terminate the 'spontaneous' element out of your romantic inclinations. If anything happens it has to be planned. Next time you feel a dream jam coming on, don't fall prey to unproductive idleness, plan a love detour.

10. Pray.

Pray as though everything depends on divine intervention. Work as though everything depends on you.

11. Start a garden.

I am inspired by Jim Rohn's book *Seasons Of Life*. In his book, he describes how we go through seasons in our pilgrimage of making a better life for ourselves. Some periods seem cold and miserable with little indication of advancement (winter), other periods (summer) are the opposite.

During the winter of a personal dream, I decided to start a tomato garden. I figured this would help me come to grips with Jim Rohn's theory. Not only did the garden supply the family with succulent tomatoes, it proved to be a very re-creative exercise. There are so many parallels between plants and dreams. Too many to name. In fact, I want you to discover the encouraging parallels for yourself. If you feel you have stalled, get out there and build a garden. It will help you process what it takes for dreams to come true.

12. Re-commit to the plan.

In order to flourish in the face of frustrating delays, keep active. Sometimes the activities, like a few of the above, are not directly related to our advancing toward our goal. Yet, because they help us avoid psychological and physical inertia from setting in, they are deemed worthy pursuits. The most important activity though, is re–committing to our plan. It is our map that keeps us directed toward our target.

When driving to a place that I have never been before, consulting the map to ensure my direction is in line with the desired destination replaces any anxious thoughts with confidence. The same principle applies when the journey toward our dream is taking longer than anticipated. Reviewing our plan restores confidence that our journey is not taking longer because we've taken a wrong turn.

Above all, in the midst of activity, remember that the most critical factor in achieving our goals is staying focussed and following the plan that we have set in place as our guide.

When dreams take their time eventuating, do not think that you've been singled out for persecution. It is an unproductive thought and plainly untrue. Instead, deal with the delay positively by making sure you have your support framework in place: a good relationship with your dream, positive mental anchors put in place, and specific positive activities to save you from idleness and self pity.

◆

THINK THE BEST

Think the best of life and people
Don't waste time thinking feeble
Make your mind behave the way
Of *who* you want to be one day
Think success before the fact
Let it shine through word and act
Visualize who you will be
Thinking shapes your destiny

— Wes Beavis —

Claiming the Prize

(The Big Day!)

◆

> *Accomplishments provide the highlights of life that illuminate our past, present, and future.*

THIRTEEN YEARS AGO, I asked Eleanor to marry me. She said no. Sometime later, I asked her again. She said maybe. This didn't feel much better than the previous no. A few months later, I asked her again. This time she said, "Um, well yes, but let's not tell anybody." At least things were progressing in the right direction, but it still wasn't quite the response I had in mind. Months later, having asked again, the angels dropped a nickel in the jukebox box of heaven which started playing our song. And we've been singing it ever since!

When I first proposed marriage to Eleanor, I expected her response to be what 'Hollywood' had conditioned me to expect. Sparks to fly, hearts to melt, and an immediate acceptance. It turned out not to resemble that at all. Convincing her to have root canal therapy would have been easier.

While the process perplexed and frustrated me, looking back I wouldn't change a thing. Having to work harder for my desire did two things. First, it increased the value in my mind of that which I sought to obtain. And second, it heightened the sensation of joy when the desire was satisfied.

There is nothing quite like the feeling of a dream coming true. The sense of fulfillment is extraordinary. The release of renewed pride in your existence is overwhelming. The excitement sends electric sensations through your spine. The attention drenches you with joy. You feel as high as a mountain, like you've broken through the clouds. You feel, at that point, invincible. You are allowed to. You've made it!

When you think about it, it's not solely the gain of what you desired that gives you this feeling. It is the knowledge that you gained what you desired because you didn't give up that magnifies the thrill.

The Wedding Banquet

I'm a great believer in celebrating the achievement of challenging endeavors. It gives people a chance to share in the thrill of the victory. It also gives others a chance to see the joy in succeeding and be encouraged to keep pursuing their own goals.

Convincing people that they need to experience more grind in life would be difficult. Surprisingly, it is also difficult persuading people they need more celebrations. It is a good thing that there is a traditional mandate for celebrations like birthdays and anniversaries. If there wasn't, we would probably let the occasions be swept away by the current of a busy life.

The chorus to one of my favorite songs goes: "*Celebrate good times, c'mon!*" (repeated several times). A fairly simple command, but one which I **need** to hear several times. What a place this world would be if we could celebrate the good times with as much passion as we report the bad times.

One of the joys of a dream coming into reality is that we are given a terrific reason to party. Unfortunately, the partying experience of too many is limited to joining with others for the common purpose of tranquilizing their senses, enabling them to forget the empty lives they lead. What a blight. Thankfully, life offers us an alternative. Succeeding in a quest grants us the opportunity to party for the sake of remembering what fantastic joy there is in succeeding.

My first profound encounter of people celebrating personal success happened some years ago. I was invited as a guest contributor to attend a business conference. There were about six hundred incredibly happy people in a banquet hall. This was my first time to a function of this nature, so I was thinking that this was either a religious revival or people were substantially inebriated. Neither was the case. There wasn't a Bible or a beer to be seen.

There was a former police officer sitting next to me. Wanting to find out what was facilitating this enthusiasm, I asked him to explain. He understood my interest. The phenomenon had, initially, also puzzled him. He had thought it was too implausible for people to be having this much fun without being drunk. His inquiry led him to discover the group's secret for happiness which he relayed to me: "If you have someone to love, something to do, and a reason to do it, you don't need to get drunk to have a good time."

This was a gathering of people who had come together to celebrate and share their achievements with each other. It was a hot-house of inspiration. Like a wedding, it was a memorable experience.

You're Allowed to be Proud

Personal pride can only be bought with the currency of honest achievement. You can have all the trophies in the world simply by going to the trophy shop and buying them. However, loading up your trophy room this way is not very satisfying. The pride one feels about a trophy is not in the trophy itself but what it represents—honest achievement. That is why cheating and success are mutually exclusive terms. The validation of success is seen in what you became in the journey.

If, in the course of the journey, you learned to cheat, any gain is inspirationally lame except to other cheaters. The ultimate celebration of a success is when your conscience is the first in line to congratulate you. I recall someone once saying: "Integrity is the place where your wealth on the outside matches your wealth on the inside." You could say the same in defining success.

Don't ever be seduced into considering shortcuts. It is sickening to find out that a sports hero has tested positive for drug use. Likewise it is nauseating when a business champion is found to have wandered into the world of embezzlement. The sourest mental taste in the mind of a positive person is discovering that someone, who was awarded the victor's crown, later had it stripped for impropriety. Remember, a trophy is a testimony to the raising of personal standards, not the compromising of them.

Short cuts are a scalpel to your confidence. One of my favorite Bible promises states: "Don't throw away your confidence, it will be richly rewarded." In this, the writer is stressing the importance of persevering. Short cuts negate the need to persevere, but it comes at the cost of your confidence. By all accounts, persevering is where confidence is born into one's life. Nothing stimulates a mood for celebrating like re-energized self-confidence.

The New You

Elevating your life to a new standard takes incredible effort. The spin-off is experiencing the exhilaration of increased confidence. "Celebrate good times, c'mon!" The new you has come into the world. In celebrating this mile-mark, you are acknowledging that you had what it took to get there. Your estimation of yourself has climbed to a level never before experienced. You have overcome what was holding you back from your moment of glory. You never need to consider yourself a member of the previous era again. You have grown. You have moved on. You have moved up!!

CONGRATULATIONS. Now, how about a little partying?

Symbolize Your Success

What constitutes a symbol of success is subject to varied opinion. Some think that certain things symbolize success while others beg to differ. Does a gold watch symbolize success? The answer lies in the person on whose wrist the watch happens to rest. The watch could have easily come to rest there as a result of theft as much as effort. Pontificating on the value of the watch all day will draw you no closer to determining whether it is a symbol of success or not.

In this day of easy credit, people can exhibit some very nice personal wares which help them look successful, but their accountants will paint you an entirely different picture. The truth is that we live in a world where we can look successful even though we are not. We can fool most people to this end. But the person who cannot be fooled is the most important of all to be considered—yourself.

True, you can parade success, but there is nothing more debilitating to your persona than to parade success you haven't earned. It is hard to display greatness that you don't have inside. You simply cannot judge a person by the clothes they wear, but you can by how confident the person looks in them. Remember, confidence is the reward for having persevered. *Confidence is the ultimate sign of success.*

Nice things will never plant within you the lasting feelings of success. Nice things can, however, reinforce feelings of success when they represent an achievement of equal value. The best symbol of success is the one which symbolizes a personal achievement of equal or greater value.

No one will be able to tell, upon a fleeting glance of your symbol, whether it attests to your being a success or not. However, over time, and in view of how your persona aligns with the symbol, they will surely know whether it is a true symbol of success.

The simple truth is: if you've earned it, it is your symbol of success. You have the right to enjoy it and wear it as a testimony to your triumph. The value someone else places on it is irrelevant, because you are not flaunting it in an effort to impress them or gain their respect. You are flaunting it as a constant reminder to yourself that there is great reward for having persevered and conquered.

In the course of a wedding ceremony, there is often the exchanging of gold rings. I recall the price of Eleanor's wedding ring being about one-hundred dollars, with mine costing even less. As pieces of jewelry, they are extremely modest in value. In what they represent, however, they are beyond value. They are irreplaceable to us because of this. They are the physical representation of something special which took place in our lives so many years ago.

The transition of our lives to a marriage commitment was a life goal for both of us. The rings symbolize and celebrate this commitment. Though we have prospered substantially since those days when we were both university students, we would never trade our wedding rings in for bigger or better ones. In over a decade, I have never had my ring removed but for a few moments. It is the physical representation of gaining the prize I had long dreamed about. She said YES. I'm still celebrating!

◆

Stage 8

Enjoying Life Together

(The Honeymoon)

◆

> The soul needs a season where concerns
> about the future are blocked out by the
> re-energizing delight that a victory brings.

I IMAGINE EVERYONE, at some time in their
life, thinks about writing a book. I do not
remember when I felt the urge to write my first
book, but I do remember feeling eleven months
pregnant with something to say. I had to give birth.
Whether there would be people willing to read
what I had written did not seem to be much of a

consideration at the time. What was most important to me was heeding the desire to structure my
thoughts into some frame that I could pass on to
people who related to life the way I did.

I'll never forget the day when the delivery
truck backed into our driveway with the first
printing of my book, *Become the Person You Dream
of Being*. There were so many boxes that we decided
that it was easier to load them into the house by
removing the window out of the third bedroom. By
the time the unloading was finished, the bedroom
was completely filled with boxes. I remember standing there with Eleanor. We were thinking about
having a another child but the enormous pile of
boxes made us realize that we had a few books to sell
if we were to use the room to house a baby.

In that moment, I felt a twinge of anxiety. A
twinge that was significantly sabotaging my thrill
for having achieved my dream in hard copy. . .
thousands of them! Instead of being excited by the
finished product, I began to worry about the next
stage. Namely, whether the book would ever make
it out of the third bedroom. Looking back, this was
an important experience to have. Through it, I
learned that we can so easily be robbed of the
blissful honeymoon experience by focussing too
soon on the next stage. Acknowledging that this
was happening, I sought to do something about it.

Eleanor and I did something that has become

a family tradition whenever we accomplish a major project. We prayed. Holding our two-year-old boy in our arms, we placed our hands upon the box nearest to us and asked God's blessing over the achievement. I don't know if this is the key to selling a lot of books, but it sure is the key to eliminating anxiety. This marked the beginning of the honeymoon for that project.

The honeymoon period is a vital follow-on from any major achievement. To rush right on to the next concern gives your spirit no time to breathe. To not take a moment to reflect on the significance of your successful quest robs your soul from experiencing the luster that a moment of glory can bring. Yes, it is possible to skip the honeymoon and get right back to the cutting edge, thinking you can 'do that' later. The problem is that we never do it later. A person who establishes this as a pattern of life usually finds their moments of reflection are done from a hospital bed rather than an exotic honeymoon location.

On the glossy surface of every achievement is an invitation to get started on the next challenge. Wisdom is knowing the right time to act upon the invitation. Feelings of anxiety more easily accompany a new challenge when you are tired from the last challenge. Don't be too quick to lock into the next endeavor when you know you're exhausted from the last one. Honeymoons are occasions for

147

blocking out concerns of the future and just purely savoring the delight of living for the moment.

Don't think that you risk losing momentum if you take such a break. On the contrary, taking time to enjoy the glow of an attained success will actually add momentum to your pilgrimage. When you stop to drink the rewards of a previous challenge, it refreshes you. A refreshed state always increases the desire to move on and tackle the next challenge.

"For everything there is a season," ancient wisdom tells us. The honeymoon is not the time to be forming the strategy for the next step, but to be basking in the glory of having succeeded in the last one. Having done this, you will be more than inspired. You'll be chaffing at the bit to get back into the race. . . Yeehaa!

Most of the time, it's hard to convince yourself to stop and enjoy a honeymoon because the euphoria of success will make you want to throw yourself at whatever is next. If you do happen to skip over the honeymoon, it will not matter as much at that point as it does further down the line. Further down the line it matters intensely.

The hardest section of any challenge is not the beginning. It is the time when the newness of the challenge wears off, and you are left with the hard task of keeping motivated when you feel otherwise. It is at this point that the experience of the honeymoon has its most powerful effect. It is easier to handle the heat of your current venture when you have a memory sweetly placed in your mind of savoring the rewards for succeeding in the last venture. Skipping your honeymoon only deprives you of valuable motivation that you will surely need down the line.

The magnitude of my honeymoon celebration directly corresponds to the magnitude of the achievement of which it represents. Having achieved one goal, I once took a group of friends out for lunch. This doesn't sound very glamorous, except that these friends were all champions in their own fields of endeavor. Getting them all in one place at one time was a feat in itself. Bigger than the thrill of being together was the knowledge that it was my dream coming true which was the catalyst for the momentous event. Looking around the table, I was surrounded by people I had admired and valued for years. This occasion of celebration was not only exceptionally enjoyable at the time, but I have continued to enjoy the memory of it many times hence.

Another honeymoon experience involved taking my family for a vacation on the other side of the planet. The sole reason was to celebrate a major achievement. When I am feeling discouraged in the midst of a current challenge; when plagued with doubts as to whether the effort is worth it, I take out a photograph of my little boy getting hugged by Mickey Mouse. It reminds me that succeeding in a past challenge enabled me to take my family to Disneyland. The honeymoon memory empowers me.

How long should a honeymoon last? A good question. Whether it is one-hundred minutes, one-hundred hours or one-hundred days, the only one who can tell how long it should be is you. You will come to a point in time on your honeymoon when you will know closure is appropriate on the last chapter, and the time has come to commence a new one. You won't need to force it. This turning point comes naturally to the motivated person.

From the Striving to the Arriving

Growing up as a child, I got caught in the familiar trap of thinking 'it will be better when'. As a four-year-old watching my older brother go off to school, I convinced myself that life would be better when I did the same. School age came and then I caught myself thinking life would be better when I became a teenager. Once a teenager, life would be better when I got my driver's license. Once licensed but very poor, I thought life would be better when I finished school and got a job. Having worked a few years, I rationalized that life would be better when I started university training. At the university, I learned that life would be better when I started my career. Once established in my career, I thought that life would be better when I got married, and so on. You know how it goes, because you have probably thought likewise.

There seems to be within the human psyche a propensity toward believing that fulfillment will come with just one more step. The truth is, fulfillment does come with one more step. But it comes in taking the step, not necessarily in where the step causes you to land.

New territory can be better than the territory we've come from, but it always comes with the discovery that it's not heaven. This is okay. It may not be heaven, but it's a much better scenario for your personal growth than never advancing beyond your current experience. Fulfillment lies not so much in the new territory gained but how the journey expands you.

Whether the grass is, or isn't greener on the other side of the valley is not the point. You cannot embark on a journey of positive discovery without arriving at your destination greater than who you were when you left. That is what is important.

Think about this the next time someone sanctimoniously likens pursuing a greener field to chasing the wind. It's not the green grass that ultimately fulfills, it's the personal growth you experience because of the journey that fulfills. The key to experiencing this growth, however, is to get up and go for the greener grass!

When You Discover Some Of The Corn Didn't Pop

Attaining an achievement always thrills the human spirit. However, it may not thrill you to the level that you had imagined. Someone once asked me, "Why is it that every victory is accompanied with some dissatisfaction about the outcome?" In probing the person for further clarification of what he was asking, I discovered that he always viewed an achievement in critical comparison of how the success could have been better. Let's face it, it happens. In fact, let's really face it, when doesn't this happen?

As a boy, I loved making popcorn. Filling the house with the sumptuous aroma of freshly-popped corn was my specialty. But something always troubled me in my pursuit of the perfect batch. Though I tried hard to avoid it, there were always a few kernels of corn at the bottom of the pan that never popped. No matter how much longer I kept the pan on the hot-plate, these kernels would not explode. Sometimes I burnt a whole batch of popcorn just trying to get the last few kernels to burst into the fullness of their potential! There is a tendency for people do the same when evaluating their achievements. They almost discard the good things for the sake of lamenting that some things failed to live up to their expectations.

Quite a few of my dreams have come true just barely scraping across the line. If I had it my way, I would prefer to soar across the line with room to spare. But with all due respect to soaring across the line with room to spare, what I have discovered is that the critical factor for long-term success is to just keep getting across the line. 'Room to spare' is irrelevant in the long run. What I have also realized is that perfectionists rarely succeed in the long run. They spend so much of their mental energy lamenting how they only got a B-grade when they wanted an A-grade, all the time depriving themselves of the glory in attaining a pass.

In the honeymoon period, you come to grips with how the result measured up to your expectation. You spend time accepting the result for what it has done. It got you across the line. Maybe not in record time or with record height, but it did do what was most valuable for you. It got you moving in the direction of achievement and growth.

While a B-grade success may be criticized by some for not being an A-grade success, those who would level this criticism at your achievement are showing their ignorance for what matters. We can not become what we want to be by remaining the way we are. It is much better to get a B-grade for an achievement, than being a flawless definition of a failure—someone who does nothing. Forget the kernels that did not pop, and enjoy nourishing yourself on those that did.

In reflecting upon your result, be careful about entering the world of comparing your results with others. Anyone who has travelled this road will tell you that it leads to an inferiority complex. There will always be someone who seems to get a better result. By focussing your mind on a comparison of your results to others, you rob yourself of the value in achieving. Achievement is meant to build your self-esteem, not provide you an opportunity to feel worse about yourself. Comparing your results to the results of others is a great exercise while you are surpassing everyone else, until you discover someone whose results make you feel inferior!

If your endeavor has transported you to a better position; caused personal growth in the process;

given you an appetite for winning, then let these things be your focus in celebrating. Use your honeymoon to get a grip on these things and squeeze them for all the rejuvenating juice they have inside. This juice will refresh you and vitalize your spirit for taking on the next challenge.

Post-project Blues

In years of pouring my heart into big projects, I have come to anticipate some post-project feelings. Usually, when you reach a pinnacle of achievement, the occasion brings feelings of excitement and elation. I have no trouble accommodating these positive sensations. Yet, it seems that included in the post-project time, is a period of experiencing feelings of a downward nature. I call these feelings the 'post-project blues.' Anyone could be forgiven for being puzzled by the timing of such feelings. Why, having achieved something dreamed about, would you feel glum afterwards?

A dream that is yet to come true energizes your spirit. It spurs you on. When the dream becomes reality, it ceases to do this. A dream achieved will be powerful in its ability to affirm your spirit, but in order for you to be spurred on to the next challenge, a new dream has to be conceived. So the period of blues is basically your subconscious experiencing the grief of change— the giving way of something special from the past in order to make way for something special for the future.

Let me illustrate this. I remember when our son David first climbed out of his cot by himself. As a father, I was elated. To me, it was the beginning of his fun and responsive 'little boy' stage. I could not understand why Eleanor did not share my excitement. The reason was not that she didn't admire his achievement, it's just that her pride was being overshadowed by something deeper. Eleanor was having to face up to the fact that a precious stage had passed. Change had happened. The baby had given way to the little boy. To any mother this is an understandable sense of loss.

Do not beat up on yourself for experiencing post-project lag. It's normal. Be not alarmed if you have a few blue moments in your honeymoon period. Expect it. When you do experience it, know that it will pass as surely as it came. Remember it is an experience which signals that things are changing, and because you cannot have growth without change, it's a very positive reminder.

◆

Stage 9

Helping Others Realize Their Dream

(Playing Cupid)

> The magnificent depth to a dream's power is
> that its influence goes beyond helping yourself.

THE LACK OF MONEY impoverishes people, but not as much as the lack of mission. I know this because years ago I became a bum for a weekend. As a bum, I experienced the truth of this statement. Let me fill you in on the details.

In the third year of my university studies the sociology lecturer gave the class the choice of two assignments: either write a three-thousand word research essay, or conduct a field experience.

To me, the latter seemed far more appealing than the option of checking into the library for three days. The thought of a field experience conjured up images of accompanying Indiana Jones on some exotic anthropological adventure. Apparently, I was the only student who thought this. The remainder of my courageous class opted for the library assignment. Upon receiving the field experience brief, I realized how prudent my class colleagues had been.

The assignment was: *To personally experience impoverishment and homelessness by living in the inner city for seventy-two hours on two dollars.* That was it.

The university was located on the perimeter of a city with a population of about four million people. I was driven downtown by the lecturer's assistant and deposited nowhere in particular. The rules of the exercise were simple. Other than what I was wearing, I was to take no clothes or bedding. Other than the two dollars allowed, I was to take no monetary devices nor was I to engage in any fund raising activities. Other than a notebook to record thoughts and experiences, I was to take nothing with me to help pass the time. I was not to make contact with anyone I knew. After the seventy-two hours, my recorded experience would be accepted as complete fulfillment of the sociology assignment. In preparation I did not shave or shower for four days. So as the lecturer's assistant bid me good luck and drove off into the congestion of city traffic, I was looking and smelling the part.

Standing on the city sidewalk, I remember musing as to why all university subject assignments couldn't be this exciting. The immediate thought following this was, "Okay I'm downtown, what should I do now?" Easy answer . . . go shopping! Well, due to my current financial situation, that meant window shopping. Over the next few hours I discovered that the enjoyment of window shopping is diminished drastically when one does not have the option to buy something. Still, it helped to pass the time. Then the shops closed. This gave way to my next discovery. Everyone I passed on the city streets was going somewhere, except for me. I had nowhere to go. I also discovered that your legs get tired when you walk the streets with nowhere to go. The fun was fading.

It was midnight. A great time of day when you are rebelling against the orthodoxy of an early night to bed. However, midnight takes on a whole new meaning when you haven't got a clue where you are going to sleep. In desperation, I went to the police station and asked the officers attending the desk where I might find somewhere to sleep. Their knowledge of places offering free lodging was limited to the point that they could not suggest anything concrete. So that's where I ended up sleeping—on the concrete of an unused shop doorway. Only sixty-five hours to go. I was very cold.

Sunrise normally means a new day. For me it meant, that for the first time in ten or so hours, I could feel warm. Heading off for the city park, I intended to lay down on a park bench and sleep in the warm rays of the sun in an effort to make up for the pitiful night of sleep. Good idea. Great idea. Fantastic idea. So good in fact, that every street hobo had in mind to do the same. Not one park bench was vacant!

"Excuse me buddy. . . you can't sleep here. I am the manager and I am here to escort you from the building." Wow, this made me mad. Having missed out on a park bench that morning and having wandered around the city aimlessly all morning, I had finally found a good place to sleep. The soft, lounge chairs of the city's movie theater lobby. How resentful I felt to have a theater manager wearing a three-piece-suit, who had obviously had a refreshing night's sleep, kick me out of his establishment! As soon as he was gone, I crept back in. This time I pushed the limits even further. I slipped right into the movie theater without paying. It was a risk worth taking. Anything to help pass the time.

Emerging from the cinema refreshed from sleeping through the movie, I started to work on how I could satisfy a ravenous hunger. I had ninety five cents left after having foolishly bought a hamburger at McDonald's on the first night. I had calculated that a train trip back to college was going to cost me sixty five cents, leaving me thirty cents to buy food for the remaining forty-eight hours. I made another major discovery; boredom and hunger make a devastating combination. How I longed to be back in the university library.

Having no success in finding a better place to sleep, I found myself back in the same shop doorway as the previous night. This night was a little different as two prostitutes were working the street near the doorway. From time to time, they would look toward me, and eventually, they headed in my direction. I remember becoming somewhat anxious as they approached. My life had not given me any significant confrontations with hookers before, and I knew with ninety-five cents jangling around in my pocket that this night was not going to change that, even had I been inclined!

They may have been prostitutes, but they acted like angels. They told me of a place where I could find a bed and a meal. That night, I thanked God for those two prostitutes and for the Salvation Army.

I wish it could be reported that I succeeded in lasting the full length of the seventy-two hour exercise. Getting to hour sixty-five and not being able to take the conditions any longer, I boarded a train bound for home.

In the days that followed, I sought to assemble my thoughts about the experiences of the weekend. I reflected on how much of our leisure and entertainment is enabled by money. I reflected on how alienated one can feel from society when you don't have a place to go or a reason to be wherever you happen to be. I reflected upon my interaction with the police, the cinema manager, and the prostitutes. In my conclusion, trying to justify my failing to reach the seventy-two hours, I laid claim to succeeding in experiencing the intention of the assignment. Then I stopped myself.

I stopped myself short of saying, "I personally experienced impoverishment and homelessness." In reality, this had not been the case. While I had experienced some of that existence, all the time I knew that at any moment, were it to get too much, I could board a train and go home. In the end, I did.

The greatest pain of that exercise was not the cold and hunger. It was coping with the boredom. Days of having nothing to do except to waste the time away, almost sent me crazy. It made me do crazy things, like steal into a movie theater.

Having no purpose to our day and no mission in our existence grates against the grain of our human nature. We are meant to dream, meant to achieve, meant to progress, meant to grow, meant to see our lives making a difference to others. The only way we can become accustomed to a life of boredom is to train ourselves to accept it as a way of life.

To be content with boredom demands that we deaden our human spirit which is otherwise designed to anticipate the delights of life's great experiences. Unfortunately, the impoverished and homeless have to do this as a matter of survival. Even more unfortunate is that some of us who are not impoverished or homeless have accustomed ourselves to a life of boredom just the same.

A person with a dream is not only saved from boredom, but has a vehicle that can rescue others from the same prison. When you have experienced a dream come true, you realize that a few minutes of 'wonderful' is much better than a lifetime of 'nothing special.' You want others to enjoy the same elevation to their spirit that you have experienced. You get frustrated when you see people with as much potential for greatness as yourself, but who are not experiencing it because, unlike you, they have not connected with a dream.

There is a principle of leadership that says, *you cannot lead someone where you have not been.*

That is why the only one who can help another person discover his or her dream is one who has been through the same experience. Society is bulging with people pregnant with potential but they are not even contemplating 'giving birth' because they do not realize they've got it in them! It is when they see another joyfully experiencing the birth of a dream, that self examination leads them to the realization that they can do the same.

Resuscitating the Human Spirit

In the movie *Pretty Woman*, actress Julia Roberts turns to Richard Gere at a poignant part of the story and says, "When people put you down long enough, you begin to believe it." These words are not only true for the individual, but also can be true for society as a whole. Because of the interest factor in bad news, it seems that bad news is all that is reported. So it goes to reason that if the dark side to society is shown for long enough, we begin to believe that society is bad. The consequence of such a belief is that we develop a 'duck for cover' survival mentality. This mentality rationalizes that a boring static life is acceptable because it is safe.

This mentality stops us from reaching out to discover the wonders of the world.

When my wife and I announced that we were moving to Los Angeles, it was interesting to hear people's responses. Some would ask, "Why would anybody in their right mind choose to live there?" It seemed that reports of riots, earthquakes, fires, mud-slides, and a few other sociological hiccups, had conditioned their minds to believe that Los Angeles was 'hell on earth.' Sometimes, we can be put off from our intentions by the cautions and concerns of others. In this case, we were not. And, as a reward, our experience has delivered a thousand marvelous compensations for living in the City of Angels. In fact, 'hell' would be knowing what we missed out on by choosing to 'duck for cover.'

Dream achievers are able to help resuscitate the spirit of our fellow man. It's an awesome task because there are so many living in self-imposed exile. But dream achievers accept the challenge, despite the odds being against them.

The story is told that early one morning, two teenagers were walking along the beach. Off in the distance they saw an elderly man engaged in the repetitive activity of throwing small objects into the ocean. Getting closer, the teenagers saw that thousands of starfish had been beached overnight.

The elderly man was attempting to save the lives of the starfish by throwing them back into the ocean before the sun's hot rays baked the life out of them.

Seeing the vast immensity of the task, the teenagers asked the elderly man, "Why bother, there are so many starfish, how could you possibly make a difference?" With that, the elderly man bent down, picked up another starfish and throwing it back into the ocean, said, "Sure made a heck of a difference to that one!"

The exciting thing about helping others discover a dream is that you are rescuing them from an existence which is doing little more than sapping the life from their creative spirit.

When you discover the forward propelling power of a dream, you first see it in view of what it can do for you. If your life has been a long pilgrimage of scratching out a meager existence, you value the power of a dream in helping you gain a better life for yourself. This is what a dream is meant to do. But its power does not stop with you. The magnificent depth to a dream's power is that its influence goes beyond just helping yourself. Duane Hulse once said: "We make a living by what we get; we make a life by what we give." A dream enables both; the capacity to get and the capacity to give.

When I received the following letter, I knew it had to be included in this book. The writer granted me permission to share his story.

Dear Wes,

I have just finished reading your book, "Become the Person You Dream of Being" and have to let you know how inspiring it is. What you wrote has helped me re-focus on a number of vital issues and has inspired me to dream bigger dreams. So often knockers condemn you by saying that dreaming and aiming high is foolish. How wrong can that be?! Your book has helped me to put the annoying uncertainty behind and go for it.

I am writing to you to share an experience that happened to me last year. I applied to join the army as a pilot. As I had been a civilian commercial pilot for two years I thought I would accomplish my ambition to fly for the military. My application went through the normal avenues and my testing was successful depending on the results of a medical examination.

At twenty-two, I was fit and healthy so I did not consider the possibility of failing the medical examination. However I did. When I was twelve I had a very minor convulsion which is what led the medical board to fail me. At the time of my convulsion I was thoroughly investigated for epilepsy or any specific disorder that would cause me future problems. The specialists said that the condition was common in adolescent males especially in response to the stress which I had been experiencing at the time of the convulsion. I was cleared.

The Army medical board did not agree. I was told that my application was unsuccessful four days before I was to join. That left me without any job because I had already trained replacements for both of my jobs. I could not go back.

I decided not to quit on the first no. I pursued my case through the local federal politician. He took it to the Director of Aviation in the Army and got the top aviation doctor on the job. This had never been done before. We were breaking new ground. It has always been the case that no one dare question the decisions of the Army. They didn't tell me that!

After four months of hounding, three neurologist visits, an EEG, two ECG's, a CT Scan, three blood tests, three hearing checks, an eye examination that lasted two hours, and twelve medicals, I was reinstated. I joined the Army on August 22nd. I am on the road to achieving my dream. Tomorrow I leave for military flight school. Out of ten-thousand applications, I am one of only twenty guys that made the course. Thank you for being such an inspiration to me. I look forward to meeting you one day.

OCDT Scott M.
Australian Air Academy

The uplift to the human spirit that a letter like this brings is priceless. Inspiring a fellow dreamer gives you the thrill of experiencing what Ralph Waldo Emerson spoke of when he said, "It is one of the most beautiful compensations of this life, that no man can sincerely try to help another without helping himself."

Discovering the Significance of a Dreamer's Life

(*Living Happily Ever After*)

◆

> *In fanning someone else's fire, you cannot help but be warmed in the process.*

IT WAS THE PRACTICE of my high school principal to write a personal reference for every graduating student. In the two years of being a student at his school, I don't remember having a conversation with him. Regardless, he came up with a reference for me. It was a fairly innocuous account of my performance but finished with the words: "Wesley is endowed with average ability and should do well at a job suited to his aptitude." At the time I remember thinking, "Wow, thanks a lot. . . hope you didn't give yourself a hernia coming up with that!" His estimation of me did not exactly build my self-esteem.

The years since then have helped me to see that he was absolutely right. Without a doubt, though he knew me not, he was on target—the description 'endowed with average ability' is still accurate. Sorry to make you wait until you have read most of the book before divulging this information to you. In fact, having gone this far, you might as well know that in many aspects of ability, this author is well below average. The truth be known, my high school principal was probably generous in his estimation. But he was not a prophet. He did not see that there was one area of life that was above average. The ability to dream. This one modest ability has driven me to success way beyond what my average ability deserves. A dream always will. One dream is all it takes to draw the extraordinary out of the ordinary.

A colleague and I were in discussions with an academic dean. We were representing some mature age students who desired to pursue a course of study at the university over which he presided. During the discussion, my colleague made the comment to the academic dean; "These people may not be the most intelligent but they're enthusiastic. . ." To this, the academic dean said something that took us both by surprise. We were under the impression that educators classically recognize ability in terms of a high I.Q. Not so with this academic dean. "Enthusiasm is intelligence," he said. "Enthusiasm unleashes the power within a person to succeed in their endeavors."

Never be intimidated by talk of intelligence quotas. A person with a high I.Q. can just as easily have these letters stand for I QUIT. To be highly intelligent and highly motivated would be the ultimate combination. But if you were only to have one, it's better to be motivated. Having drive leads one to higher intelligence, whereas intelligence rarely leads a person to be more motivated. The significance of a dreamer's life is that, whatever their level of ability, their dreams motivate them to achieve beyond it.

Enabled To Be Stable

Oliver Wendell Holmes Jr. once said, "It's not where you are standing, but the direction that you're heading which matters." A dreamer's life will always be a trajectory to significance because they have set their direction toward it. I remember being with friends and watching the video of the movie *Rudy*. It was a movie based on the life of Daniel E. "Rudy" Ruettiger, whose dream in life was to play football for the University of Notre Dame. At five-foot and a few inches and not much heavier than a hundred pounds, people laughed at his ambition. Legitimate sources said he had virtually no chance of being a Notre Dame football player.

The closest Rudy got to the team was in being selected for the practice squad. His role was to give the starting players something to beat up on. The practice squad's greatest value to the coaches was in the fact that if a member of the practice squad was hurt, it was of no concern for the coaches. Though his role was esteemed little more than a a human punching bag, Rudy never missed a practice in four long years. Always hoping that one day he would get a chance to play on the starting team, most of the movie is about Rudy trying to keep his dream alive. Eventually his moment came. Literally, it was only a moment. It was the last minute of the last game of his last season attending Notre Dame.

After the movie, we sat around discussing whether one minute of playing time was worth four years of agonizing effort. One of the group made the comment, "I worry about Rudy being caught up in a dream-world." A fair enough comment, but what would have been the alternative? Should he have taken better inventory of his abilities and channeled his energies in another direction? Maybe he would have found something more suited about which to be passionate. Maybe he would not have. The truth is, no one will know. What we can know is that his dream rescued him from a life of possible nothingness and all the instability that such a life induces.

When riding a bike, you can't maintain stability by standing still. Stability comes when you get on the move. True, Rudy's dream caused an intensive struggle, but it also gave him a mission in life. A mission in life has a way of establishing personal stability despite the roller-coaster ride of emotions which the mission may induce. I would argue that investment in your dream is worth it, even if the complete fulfillment of your dream doesn't materialize. When you consider the alternative of doing nothing, one is always better off for having tried to make their dreams their reality.

Shifting Desires

An airplane pilot was flying over a picturesque lake in the mountains. Turning to his crew he said, "When I was young, I fished on that lake. I would sit in the boat and every time a plane flew over, I would dream of one day flying. Now I fly over that lake and wish I were down there fishing."

Over the course of our life, our desires change. What is a strong personal desire at one point in your life will not always remain a strong desire. Some may feel that negates the value of the dream in the long run. These people might say, "If I wait it out, the desire will pass, thus saving myself the pressure of trying to make the dream come true."

Yes, if you 'wait it out' the desire will pass. So will your life, leaving you with a one-dimensional, monotoned legacy as testimony to your existence. Needless to say, you would be an inspiration to fewer people than you could have been. Allowing your dreams and visions to influence your destiny is like trading in your charcoal pencil on a set of paint bombs. The canvas of your life becomes less a demonstration of bland control and more an expression of excitement, vitality, creativity and the unexpected. Even though it lends itself to more possible mess, it is still better and more inspirational.

Dreams That Raise the Living

Years ago, I was asked to officiate a funeral. Such a request comes periodically when you're a pastor. The years had given me ample opportunities to serve in this manner, but I will never forget this one particular funeral. It was the last one I did. It was the one that led me to decide never to officiate another funeral in my life.

Sadly, an elderly man unable to cope with the loneliness of the years since losing his wife, ended his own life. I was called in by the funeral director who informed me that his death was self-inflicted and that the only known next of kin was a step-daughter. This was going to be a tougher funeral than usual. I organized a meeting with the step-daughter in order to piece together a thoughtful eulogy. The funeral was the next day.

As was service procedure for the placement of the next of kin, the step-daughter took her place in the front row of the chapel.

If it is not appropriate to say of funerals that things were going well, at least you could say that things were going according to plan. I had concluded the eulogy and proceeded to address the next of kin with some words of comfort. Pastoral comments always called for direct visual contact with those to whom the remarks were being addressed. My attention was directed to the under-standably emotional step-daughter, while the rest of the congregation looked on.

Suddenly the somber atmosphere was inter-rupted. "What about me?" the words boomed from somewhere in the back of the chapel. I couldn't believe my ears. Someone was hi-jacking my funeral service. "Excuse me sir," I asked, "what about you?"

In my mind I was thinking, "You're not dead yet, but I could arrange it if you want to keep this up!"

His reply absolutely swamped me. "I was his brother, don't I matter?" I looked at the funeral director who was standing at the rear of the chapel looking as uncomfortable as I was. Neither he nor I had any idea that this man had a brother, let alone that he'd be sitting there incognito.

I do not recall how I ever recovered from that embarrassing situation to conclude the service. What I will never forget, was thinking as I walked to my car, "That is the last funeral I'll be doing." That day I made a monumental decision. If tough situations were to be encountered, I would much rather them be the result of trying to raise the living rather than sending off the dead.

Since then, I have dedicated myself to being in the army of people who spend their lives helping others come alive to their potential.

Seeing your life have a positive impact in the life of another is one of the most deeply gratifying experiences you'll ever have. It grants significance to your existence. It gives you the feeling that you have been personally responsible for leaving a positive mark on humanity. There is little else that fuels the fire of the human spirit than to catch a glimpse of your own significance within another's life.

I'll never forget the person that showed me how to play my first notes on the piano. Nor the person who wrote the first inspirational book I read. Nor the first person I recall saying to me, "I believe in you." I'll never forget the person that first shared with me God's love. These people are immortalized in me. I carry a piece of their life entwined in mine. They share in my destiny. They are jointly responsible for it!

When we stop to consider it, our personal history is punctuated with people who have positively helped to shape our lives. The greatest honor we can bestow upon those people is to make our lives a tribute to their decision to stop and pour a little of themselves into us.

I am inspired by the story of a young boy who was trapped in a burning building. His calls for help were heeded by a man passing by. Risking his own life, the man broke through a locked door and rescued the boy. Once outside and having made sure that the boy was alright, the man turned and walked away. Seeing his rescuer walking off into the distance, the boy called out, "Hey mister, you saved my life. What can I do for you?" The man paused, turned around and simply said, "Young man, live a life worth saving."

Fanning The Flame Of Someone Else's Fire

A recent episode of the popular television drama 'ER' (Emergency Room), featured the theme of one doctor's struggle to separate his personal feelings from the life and death tasks he faced every day. In one poignant scene, a colleague friend said to him, ". . .there are people out there in desperate need. Helping them is more important than how we feel." What an incredible statement! Dreamers will always face the temptation to abort their mission. Feelings will often lead the assault. What stops you and me from caving into defeat comes down to whether we value our feelings over the real needs of others.

Serving others at the expense of one's own feelings does two things. First, it changes your feelings. And then, it changes you. It promotes you to a level of greatness which, by pandering to your emotions, you could never achieve. Choosing to attend to the needs of others over your own does not come naturally. We are inclined by nature to be selfish. To serve others requires one to deny the natural inclination and draw strength from higher values.

Unfortunately, the idea of being a servant conjures up images of some pathetic butler whose whole purpose in life is to facilitate the domestic whims of some elitist baron. Allowing this picture of servanthood to become the defining image is a distortion. Being a servant is not being a doormat. Contrary to popular opinion, it is not a position of weakness, but one of displayed strength.

Serving ourselves comes easily. Serving others takes more effort. It's harder because you have to defy natural inclinations to do so. But any time one chooses the harder road, they become stronger in character and nobility. To these people is extended the gift of significance. Their lives stand testimony to the fact that by fanning someone else's fire, you cannot help but be warmed in the process.

The Giving Of The Blessing

You and I know that *not* everyone will succeed. Only those who desire success will succeed. The challenge is figuring out which ones have no desire and which ones have desire that has been lost in some cavernous pothole deep within their lives. To this end, I am constantly being surprised. People I would have thought were hopeless cases have gone on to prove me wrong by becoming impassioned for advancement. Others I considered to be 'primed for the presidency' have proven me wrong by never living up to being voted 'most likely to succeed.'

Though at times I wish there was a way to foretell a person's potential destiny, I know it's better for humanity that we can not. It saves us from committing the error of judging, categorizing, then relegating people to our self-established scrap heap. It also keeps life interesting. We may think a person is dead to development, when in reality they are just dormant. This person's resurrection may be hinging on someone just saying: "I believe in you" or "I love you" or "Let's do this together."

A person may never ignite. Or, they may not ignite at that point, but you have been instrumental in bringing them closer to combustion and great success. Then again, their lives may have come to the point where your blessing is the spark that releases their hibernating energy into a raging fire. You never know what a person's potential is. So what do you do? Simply treat everyone you meet as a winner in the making, needing just one more spark—YOURS!

"One More Spark Before I Go, Son"

Before I left home to attend college, my father sat me down for some paternal counsel. It was advice which I accepted in view of my enormous respect for him, but nonetheless, it was advice I was reluctant to take. He suggested giving up something I loved. Music. Up until that point in my life, I had been an enthusiastic musician and a budding songwriter. There was not an aspect of my life where I could not, in some way, involve the guitar or piano. Even in my scholastic endeavors, assembling important information into a song greatly assisted me to recall information. Can you imagine sitting next to someone singing his way through an exam?

183

Dad approved of my musical inclinations as a positive source of recreation to keep me occupied through the difficult adolescent years. However, he also believed that college would be the time when I should 'hang up the gloves' on these musical inclinations so I could more fully concentrate on training for a career. On this occasion, I decided to take his advice. In setting up my room on the campus, I slid my guitar under the bed, and with it my song-writing impulses. There it stayed for a few years, as I believed that my father's counsel was right.

As the years went by, I began to realize that music was not a passing interest for me. The desire to compose gave rise to being involved more and more in the world of music. In doing so, I realized it was acting contrary to Dad's counsel. To rationalize this, I concluded that my adult status deemed it was time for me to do what I felt was right. From then on, I just considered this side of my life as something where Dad and I would disagree.

It is a dilemma when those you love do not approve of something you love doing. I was not 'hung-up' on needing the approval of my father, but then again my respect for him made me want his approval. On the whole, we communicated very well. When given the opportunity, we would talk for hours about everything, except music. I was reluctant to divulge anything to do with that area of my life. I was content to 'let sleeping dogs lie' so to speak, fearing that bringing up the subject might freshen the disagreement. Then one day it all changed.

Eleanor and I had travelled three-thousand miles to where my parents lived, in order to attend a family occasion. The vast distance between our respective homes meant that our visits were infrequent, so Eleanor and I stayed a few extra days and went away on a vacation with Dad and Mom. We stayed in a country motel and simply enjoyed each other's company until it was time to return home. It was a four hour car trip back to my parent's house, and with Eleanor and my mother asleep, Dad and I started talking. I just felt there would be no better time to bring up the subject with him.

I was honest with Dad in saying I had tried to discard the desire to be a songwriter. I told him of feeling disconnected in sharing with him that part of my life. He paused before answering. Then in the most humble manner, he answered: "Son, in the years since we had that discussion, I have grown to realize that what you have in your heart has been put there by God. He put it there for you to use, so use it. It would be wrong for me or anyone else to counsel you to do otherwise. Son. . . give it all you've got. You have my blessing."

Two hours later, I burst through the front door of the house to find my mother crying in the kitchen. My father's lifeless body was lying next to her. A massive heart attack had taken him away.

For twenty-four years, I was privileged to be his son. I will be forever thankful that the last words I recall my father saying to me have empowered me to persue my dreams. "Son, give it all you've got. You have my blessing." My goal remains: to live a life worthy of that blessing.

If we desire it, we too can inspire the lives of others, not only now, but long after our physical presence is gone. That is the potential, power, and significance of a dreamer's life. I am sure you agree, a significant life is a dream well worth dating.

◆

TODAY IS THE START

Today is the start
So today I've begun
To throw my heart into doing
What I'm compelled to become
For I have realized
My potential to be
Has been put there by God
As His dream for me

— Wes Beavis —

About the Author

Wes Beavis was born in Australia and now lives in the United States with his wife Eleanor, and their two sons, David and Zachary.

◆